To Glenda,
In appropriate friendship
began at the Water fountain at the NLS!

Border Dance

Ian

Border Dance

A Study in Contrasts and Conflict
and How to Resolve Them

JIMI CALHOUN

Foreword by Brian D. McLaren

CASCADE *Books* · Eugene, Oregon

BORDER DANCE
A Study in Contrasts and Conflict and How to Resolve Them

Cascade Books
An Imprint of Wipf and Stock Publishers
199 W. 8th Ave., Suite 3
Eugene, OR 97401

www.wipfandstock.com

PAPERBACK ISBN: 978-1-6667-3853-7
HARDCOVER ISBN: 978-1-6667-9937-8
EBOOK ISBN: 978-1-6667-9938-5

Cataloguing-in-Publication data:

Names: Calhoun, Jimi, author. | McLaren, Brian D., foreword.

Title: Border dance : a study in contrasts and conflict and how to resolve them / Jimi Calhoun; foreword by Brian D. McLaren.

Description: Eugene, OR: Cascade Books, 2023 | Includes bibliographical references.

Identifiers: ISBN 978-1-6667-3853-7 (paperback) | ISBN 978-1-6667-9937-8 (hardcover) | ISBN 978-1-6667-9938-5 (ebook)

Subjects: LCSH: Race relations—Religious aspects—Christianity. | Dance—History. | Race awareness.

Classification: E185.615 C265 2023 (paperback) | E185.615 (ebook)

10/06/23

Dedicated to Clifford Coulter, Isabel Whyte, Dennis Marcellino, Annette Louise Grable, and Rich Miller

In loving memory of William and Xanthyne Calhoun and Jules and Lorraine Brown

Contents

SECTION THREE | RELIGION

Foreword

ONE OF THE GREAT joys and privileges of my life was the opportunity to work for several years with Jimi Calhoun.

We shared a vocation as pastors and preachers, and we also shared a love for music. I was an amateur who played acoustic guitar and wrote songs, but Jimi was a pro. As a world-class bassist, he toured and recorded with funk, blues, jazz, and rock groups like Creation, Dr. John, Parliament Funkadelic, and Buddy Miles. He wasn't one to talk much about himself, but I can't count how many times I'd mention a famous musician of the sixties and seventies, and Jimi would casually mention performing, jamming, or hanging out with him or her.

In addition to pastoring, preaching, and playing music, Jimi and I shared a love for history, science, art, culture and . . . really, just about everything, because we both have inborn curiosity and a lifelong desire to learn.

One more thing we have in common: skin color.

By that I mean that both of our skins have color. Mine is pale, a bit reddish perhaps. His is brown. Even though many people would classify us as different, even opposite, neither of us is simply coal black or snow white. Our skins have color, in between—and much more interesting than—the simplistic and inaccurate categories of black and white. (Jimi explores this idea more in chapter 7.)

I surfed around on the internet and found several fascinating skin tone charts. Unsurprisingly, makeup companies made the most fine-tuned ones. The best match I could find for me was called "serene peach," and for Jimi, "saddle brown."

The simplistic binary of blackness and whiteness, we both know, is a social construction.

Jimi believes that "there is only one race, the human race," and one of the ways we can move beyond the vicious lie of racism is to face that truth.

Our differences, he suggests, are matters of culture, not race, and cultural differences invite us—not to fight or fear each other—but to come together and dance.

In some of his previous books, Jimi focused on the power of music to invite us into harmony. In this new book, he focuses on the power of dance.

He interweaves the history of dance and the history of racism . . . the role of dance in culture and the role of racism in economics and politics. He follows dance across history and around the globe, from the Americas and Europe to Africa and Asia. If you're like me, by the time you're halfway through the book, you'll be more fascinated by dance than you've ever been, and you'll suspect that maybe the way for us to move beyond the ingrained racist habits of the past will be more like learning to dance than winning an argument or passing a law.

I grew up in a form of Christianity that believed dancing (like drinking and smoking) was a sin. So for many years, I was a wallflower, watching others have fun, stuck in what Thomas Merton called an "awful solemnity" of "strange finalities," secretly wishing I could join in. Eventually I got up my courage, and even though all my dance moves resembled the robot, I had fun.

When Jimi invites us to see the rich cultural diversity of dance, he helps us break out of our "awful solemnity" and "strange finalities." He knows there is a grand cosmic dance, and in that dance, humanly constructed borders of race, religion, and class shouldn't keep us apart. Instead, we should kick up our heels and erase them with our dancing feet.

Thomas Merton's words on dance in *New Seeds of Contemplation* (New Directions, 1949) seem like a fitting prelude to the beautiful book you're about to read by my colleague and friend Jimi Calhoun:

> . . . the Lord plays and diverts Himself in the garden of His creation, and if we could let go of our own obsession with what we think is the meaning of it all, we might be able to hear His call and follow Him in His mysterious, cosmic dance. We do not have to go very far to catch echoes of that game, and of that dancing. When we are alone on a starlit night; when by chance we see the migrating birds in autumn descending on a grove of junipers to rest and eat; when we see children in a moment when they are really children; when we know love in our own hearts; or when, like the Japanese poet Bashō we hear an old frog land in a quiet pond with a solitary splash—at such times the awakening, the turning inside out of all values, the "newness," the emptiness and the purity of vision that make themselves evident, provide a glimpse of the cosmic dance.

For the world and time are the dance of the Lord in emptiness. The silence of the spheres is the music of a wedding feast. The more we persist in misunderstanding the phenomena of life, the more we analyze them out into strange finalities and complex purposes of our own, the more we involve ourselves in sadness, absurdity and despair. But it does not matter much, because no despair of ours can alter the reality of things; or stain the joy of the cosmic dance which is always there. Indeed, we are in the midst of it, and it is in the midst of us, for it beats in our very blood, whether we want it to or not.

Yet the fact remains that we are invited to forget ourselves on purpose, cast our awful solemnity to the winds and join in the general dance.

I will leave you with this encouragement from Shakespeare (*The Winter's Tale* 4.4): "When you do dance I wish you a new wave of the sea, that you ever do nothing but that . . ."

Brian D. McLaren

Acknowledgments

IN LOVING GRATITUDE, I thank my Brown angel, Julaine Calhoun, whose unwavering love and support made this book possible. Thank you to all the family members who have extended unconditional love throughout these many years. With deepest gratitude I thank Robert, Kimberly, and Ian Watson-Hemphill for their supportive friendship and understanding. I thank the Hoffman family for always being there. Thank you to Kate Henderson for your tenderhearted care over long years. And a heartfelt appreciation to Janie and Sterling Spell, and the Rev. Dr. Stephen Kinney.

I would like to express my gratitude to the many friends in the Iona Community. A shout out to the Moore and Gordon small groups that provided a place to call home. To Rodney Clapp, who has been the perfect mentor and guide throughout my writing career, thank you. To Paul Louis Metzger and Mariko Metzger, your lives exemplify faith, hope, and love. Thanks to the friends who have offered encouragement along the way: the Nazarians, Andersons, Doyals, Shanahans, Christensons, Frantanduanos, Ermeavs, Grables, Selvas, Bells, and the Woolery-Prices. Special thanks to Scotty Varneau, Nancy Mustard, Susan Lawson, and Jeanne Adams. Lastly, to all of the wonderfully talented musicians I have recorded and toured with, thank you for keeping the dance alive.

Prologue

Dissolving Social Borders

DURING TIMES OF GLOBAL uncertainty, what can be done to reduce tensions and cross the social borders between nationalism, race, and religion? Allow me to share one answer that may surprise you: dance! Dance? Stay with me. What do science, music, theology, and dance have in common? Each of these disciplines thrives in the unknown. Correspondingly, each of them requires imagination, experimentation, and innovation to execute their aims. And the word *dance* has more applications than you may realize. As you will see, "dance interweaves with other aspects of human life such as communication and learning, belief systems, social relations, political dynamics, loving and fighting."[1] These diverse disciplines came together to help produce the dance of life.

With this book, I hope to show that the best solutions to social border conflict need not come through legislation or consensus. Some of the most disturbing ideas in history have been implemented due to votes or popular opinion, a.k.a. mass justification. I propose that better solutions to conflict can come from a peacemaking process born of dance.

Many people believe that for a nation to exist it is necessary to have clearly defined borders. That human flourishing depends on racial designations to identify who is "like us." And that faithfulness to God requires hard-and-fast boundaries to maintain religious purity. This book challenges you to rethink borders of this type by studying dance. I argue that dancing across borders is a viable method of resolving conflict. I can say this because "dance is an activity that animates every dimension of our bodily selves . . . It is vital for the health and well-being of our emotional, intellectual, and

1. Hanna, *To Dance Is Human*, 1.

1

spiritual selves."[2] Life places countless boundaries before you, and dance can help dissolve each of them.

I make three assumptions about social borders in this book. The first is that Americans take pride in being a citizen of the United States of America and are fiercely loyal to it. The second is that most of our intimate relationships run along racial lines. The third is that most Americans live out their spirituality through participation in one of the three Abrahamic faiths. Those religions are Judaism, Christianity, and Islam. It is regrettable that many accept religious fragmentation as normal. That happens because they believe God has only spoken to one group of people and in only one way. But Christianity is more expansive than that. And here is why. According to one prominent theologian, our faith is "a narrative of God's work in creation and history."[3] To put this in context, over 100 billion people have lived and died throughout history and scientists tell us the universe is still expanding. To state the obvious, the purview of God is vast.

For this reason, we will discuss portions of the histories of nationalism, race, and religion in the context of dance. I contend that the "study of the past . . . is simultaneously of and about past and future."[4] History is a necessary component of this study. This is due to the fact that border walls of separation didn't appear overnight. Like the Great Wall of China, social borders were built ideological brick by ideological brick over hundreds of years. For example, Tim Marshall wrote of a time he visited China in his book *The Age of Walls*. He suggests that as grand an achievement as the wall was, it never succeeded in keeping people out. I argue this is not true of the walls we build inside our hearts. We're all experts at keeping people outside of them. This is so because establishing boundaries is simpler than cultivating love.

In the following pages I will present three pictures of how human beings live. They are how we live politically, culturally, and spiritually. In this book, the concept of race is interchangeable with that of culture. To be clear, there is only one race, the human race. That means the differences in how people live are cultural and not "racial." Consequently, what many call racial conflict is really a matter of different cultures colliding. To counterbalance that, I will show ways to let go of the tendency to see all aspects of life politically and racially. You will then be encouraged to broaden your spiritual horizons.

---

2. Lamothe, *Why We Dance*, 3.

3. Oden, *How Africa Shaped the Christian Mind*, 14.

4. Dils and Albright, *Moving History/Dancing Cultures*, xiv.

For starters, let us turn to Russian-American sociologist Pitirim Sorokin for insight. We all know that shoes are an integral part of dance. Sorokin suggests that we ignore our nationalistic shoes until danger approaches. We do not pay attention to our ethnic-cultural shoes until somebody steps on them. And we do not pay much attention to our spiritual shoes until we realize some beliefs no longer fit. Pretty accurate, isn't it?

WHY DANCE?

Why the focus on dance? First of all, the great moral awakening that followed the George Floyd incident has faded. I believe it needs to be rebooted. Secondly, race is an intricate issue that goes beyond violence. I wanted to open a conversation that focused more on the social conflict aspect. In my view, violence is an outgrowth of that conflict, not the root of it. Lastly, I chose dance as a backdrop for this reason: Every society has its own set of cultural norms and values. Dance can reflect those norms and values. Additionally, social borders can be breached and reconfigured through dance. Anthropologist Judith Lynn Hanna writes, "Human groups identify themselves and maintain their boundaries . . . by using signs already in existence."[5] Similarly, many of us erect social walls based on stereotypes and myths that are widely accepted. We can either tear down the barriers that people create, or we can dance around them.

As Hanna accurately observes, "Dance may function in the same way as speech."[6] We use many kinds of words when we speak, don't we? Similarly, dance allows a person a variety of ways to communicate. However, unlike speech, dance communicates beyond words because it sets the mind and heart free. Dancing opens up the floor for "risk-free" intimacies. For many, it is easy to ask a stranger to dance. That is because dancing extends beyond the self. As Walter Terry writes, "We know that order and harmony and social contact do exist and if they are attainable for dancers they should certainly be attainable for everyone else."[7]

CULTURE AND IDENTITY

Today nationalism is understood to be the glue that holds people groups together. But in a nation-state, a dominant culture can emerge that has little or

5. Hanna, *To Dance Is Human*, 83.

6. Hanna, *To Dance Is Human*, 83.

7. Terry, *Invitation to Dance*, 6.

no tolerance for opposing views. What happens if the majority in a nation-state engages in conduct that a marginalized group believes to be wrong or immoral? Conflict! Since the powerful are rarely willing to have their actions scrutinized or criticized by those with less power, problems arise. This book shows how that leaves people outside the seat of power without access to justice. But consider this: "It is the exercise of human justice that lends harmony to society and creation as a whole, whereas injustice upsets this harmony."[8] Resolving conflict is more than pursuing justice in a court of law or legislature. Moral hair-splitting? Absolutely not! Pursuing justice the legal route apart from stamping out injustice can solve one problem while creating another. For solutions to last, they must include eliminating injustice in all its forms.

POWER AND OTHERNESS

According to psychologist Geert Hofstede, "One of the most salient aspects of inequality is the degree of power each person exerts or can exert over other persons."[9] And author Terry Eagleton has shared one of the most verifiable truths of all time: "power loathes weakness."[10] Historically, antipathy toward the weaker has caused conflict, followed by dehumanization. Those with power classify the less powerful on their terms. Then they assign them to a place outside the borders of acceptance. That is how many "isms," like racism and others, come to be. Anthropologist Clifford Gertz uncovered a tool the powerful use to validate their favored status. According to Angela Saini, Gertz suggests "man is an animal suspended in webs of significance that he himself has spun."[11] Through self-deception, the powerful convince themselves of an inherent, or God-given, right to power. This book refutes the entire premise. I strongly argue that the best power to have is the power to love.

GET READY

"Get Ready" is a song recorded by two popular Motown acts. One version is by a rhythm and blues vocal group named The Temptations. The second is a version by a rock band called Rare Earth. I was a member of that

---

8. Brock, *Luminous Eye*, 166.

9. Hofstede-insights.com, "Country Comparison," lines 15–17.

10. Eagleton, *Evil*, 100.

11. Saini, *Superior*, 25.

platinum-selling band at one time. One day both groups happened to be traveling on the same flight. The Temptations' lead singer Dennis Edwards and I began a conversation about music. I joked that when we got to our next gig, we would perform the same song in entirely different ways. Dennis complained that while performing "Get Ready," he has to dance and sing, "but when you play it, you can simply stand there and play the bass." I reminded him that they had the bigger hit, and that is the "end of the story."

The truth is, I was wrong because Rare Earth's version actually sold more records. But why let something like a fact spoil a good conversation on an airplane? Let me address getting ready. Dance instructor Cynthia Winton-Henry artfully states, "Preparation is good, but nothing replaces the act of actually beginning to move."[12] Despite its title, this is not a book devoted to finding simple solutions to all of our social problems. However, it will challenge you to rethink some things. And it will prepare your heart to love others. To do that, I encourage you to read through an empathetic lens.

The stories you are about to read will play out like partner dances. These dances require a leader and a follower, i.e., an aggressor and a recipient. Empathetic reading requires that you place yourself in the shoes of the recipients, the people who suffered due to the aggressive actions of others. The pages you are about to read will move you to share God's peace with those you have had little contact with in the past. Get ready!

---

12. Winton-Henry, *Dance—the Sacred Art*, 31.

CHAPTER 1

Introduction

"Dance first. Think later. It is the natural order."[1]

—SAMUEL BECKETT

INITIALLY, THE GOOD NEWS of God was transmitted via vernacular speech, i.e., Hebrew, Greek, and Latin. Similarly, the vernacular dances of cultures around the world display the oneness of humanity. It was American vernacular dance that framed my journey into the world of professional music-making. I cut my teeth on rock and roll music during the postwar dance boom of the 1960s. The dance music I played derived its style from the unique blend of that specific culture. What follows is a partial list of the dance styles native to the US: "Hip-Hop, Tap Dance, and its derivative Rock and Roll."[2] Americans are truly a dancing people. The authors of *Jazz Dance* concede, "The subject of vernacular dance is so vast that . . . we gave up the idea of telling the whole story."[3] However, dance is useful in ways other than storytelling. That is because it can communicate without ever running out of words.

Now I will take you on a journey back to the beginnings of the many dances influenced by rock and roll. As a starting point, let us look at a time in Western history when a Greek god named Dionysus was at the peak of his popularity. Dionysus was the son of Zeus, "ruler, protector, and father

---

1. Goodreads.com, "Samuel Beckett."

2. Danceask.net, "Top USA/American Origin Dance Forms," line 12.

3. Stearns and Stearns, *Jazz Dance*, xvii.

of all gods and humans."[4] A party-like atmosphere surrounded his worship. Best-selling author Barbara Ehrenreich writes, "With his long hair . . . and his promise of ecstasy, Dionysus was the first rock star."[5] The Dionysian experience consisted of a mix of "drunkenness and madness . . . enthusiasm and ecstasy . . . [and] music is the most Dionysian of the arts."[6] Dionysus, like every other rock star, "journeyed far and wide. Everywhere he went he planted vines and taught the people viniculture [normalized drinking]."[7] The Dionysian influence transcended physical boundaries in the same way dance culture has today.

There was also a belief within the Dionysus cult that "dance was an instrument with which the dancer could achieve a closer communion with divinity by entering into a state of rapture."[8] Similar beliefs were held by people in distant geographies, including China and Africa. That demonstrates dance's history of crossing borders. Correspondingly, touring musicians regularly crossed physical and cultural boundaries. Many times our audiences would regard our performances as a spiritual experience. Sex, drugs, and rock and roll were the credos of the day for both the touring musicians and festivalgoers. I watched people from every background free themselves of whatever separated them culturally and dance with each other.

Dance is able to cross cultural and spiritual boundaries because you access it through all the senses, not just cerebrally. You only need to see African worship to get that. If you have, you understand that dance involves more than the mind. The reason for that is the body and soul participate in it equally. During my music career it became clear that dance is a spiritual practice in its own right. Early Christian leaders called the fathers of the church acknowledged such possibilities. They distinguished between "knowledge in the ordinary sense . . . and spiritual knowledge, which by its function transcends the natural realm."[9] Martha Graham, once named dancer of the century by *Time* magazine, explains why. It is because "Dance is an absolute. It is not knowledge about something, but is knowledge itself."[10]

---

4. Britannica.com, "Zeus," line 6.

5. Ehrenreich, *Dancing in the Streets*, 41.

6. Faculty.fiu.edu, "Apollonian/Dionysian Dichotomy," line 10.

7. Rijksmuseum.nl, "Dionysus/Bacchus," line 3.

8. Encyclopedia.com, "Dionysian Dance."

9. Nesteruck, *Light from the East*, 53.

10. Lamothe, *Why We Dance*, 59.

The environment where this kind of knowledge spreads is not in the halls of academia but in thousands of dance halls, nightclubs, and festivals. The Bickershaw Festival in England is one example of this. I had the privilege of performing at that festival with Dr. John. One attender, Elvis Costello, who would later achieve worldwide fame, "stood in the mud amazed by the five-hour set from the Grateful Dead, the performance which convinced him he should start a band."[11] I was there, and I watched kids dance and slosh around the rain-soaked field, entirely mesmerized by the music of the Grateful Dead. That was what a rock festival was like, and it echoes the Dionysian festivals of ancient Greece.

I am from the San Francisco Bay Area. That is where Grateful Dead fans developed a free-form dance style during the hippie era. However, when the hippie era ended, that dance style fell out of favor with everyone except Grateful Dead fans called Deadheads. These are people who travel to see as many "Dead" shows as possible. A Grateful Dead show "is a place where community is developed through the communal attainment of mystical states and that those who are most open to transforming their consciousness in the concert environment through dance, hallucinogens and music tend to become devoted Deadheads."[12]

If you are ever curious about what that looked like, go to YouTube and type in "Grateful Dead live."[13] Watch the audience in the video. You will see people dancing without another dancer close to them. As with the Dionysian experience, Deadheads are a coterie of thrill seekers "in the moment" with the music. Concertgoers and church attenders alike can learn much from Deadheads. That is because "they show how subcultures both challenge and resist the dominant culture."[14] Some argue that today's church mimics the dominant culture a little too closely. In other words, faith communities exist to maintain the status quo, not to influence or transcend it.

By following the band around, Deadheads built a community of strangers. It would be cool if we could say that about churches. To illustrate what it means to follow the Dead, basketball star Bill Walton says he attended over 650 Grateful Dead shows. In contrast, the church opts for programs and events that happen in short bursts. One element missing in cross-cultural ministry is a commitment to investing time.

That raises the following question: How can someone say they love a people group they feel uncomfortable spending time with? Isn't that a

---

11. Wikipedia.org, "Bickershaw Festival," para. 3, line 2.

12. Haenfler.sites.grinnell.edu, "Subcultures and Sociology," para. 7, line 8.

13 Or go here: https://www.youtube.com/watch?v=o2h2NuFkVA0.

14. Haenfler.sites.grinnell.edu, "Subcultures and Sociology," para. 10, line 1.

contradiction? My missionary experience taught me these valuable lessons. Visiting someone on the margins is not the same as *being* marginalized. This is why brief glimpses into the lives of marginalized people do not have much impact on those doing the visiting. That is because spending a minimal amount of time is insufficient to sense the others' realities. For that to happen, one needs to cross a border and stay awhile.

"This world we live in is the dance of the creator."[15]

MICHAEL JACKSON

Dance and music are inextricably linked, but which of these elements contributes most to the enjoyment of the other? If you have sung in the shower, you have engaged in music without dancing. And if you have ever pumped a fist at the sound of good news, you have danced without music. However, when you're ready to party, you probably won't have a successful dance without music.

What is significant about music is that "every culture develops melodies, rhythms, and instruments to express a range of emotions—happiness, pride, sorrow, reflection, and love."[16] That is also true of dance. There is one other word I would add to that list, and that is responsiveness. According to the Oxford dictionary, the adjective form can mean "reacting quickly and positively."[17] In both dance and music, response is a key component of success. And learning how to respond creatively to change is a crucial part of the premise of this book.

I spent thirteen years of my life playing dance music nationally and internationally. While performing at festivals and nightclubs it was fun to watch people dance in sync with my bass, and I would feel at one with them. At other times the dancer's sense of time was kind of abstract. So abstract I wondered if they heard what I was playing and, if so, if they understood it. There is a corollary to life in all of this, isn't there? When the Europeans first encountered the world's darker-skinned people they reacted quickly, but not positively, to their "strange" (to them) customs. They did not understand the cultures and did not know what they saw. Consequently, they called the festivals and rites of passage enjoyed by these darker-skinned people primitive or savage.

The Europeans targeted dance because they couldn't appreciate the creativity of the African people. Even today, many inside and outside

15. Goodreads.com, "Michael Jackson."
16. Nh.gov, "Folk Life," line 1.
17. Lexico.com, "Responsive."

Christianity react negatively to seeing darker-skinned people dancing. They see vulgarity. For example, this was said about one particular style in a book about the history of dance: "From the lowest levels of mankind, indeed to the apes, it [the dances of darker-skinned people] reaches into the rustic dances of higher cultures."[18] Many African dances had also taken root in Latin America. They included the samba, the rumba, and the tango. When describing a dance named the tango, the author writes, "It is no pure Negro dance, and owes its best qualities to the unusual dance talents of the Spaniard."[19] That qualifier was necessary because "many negro dances seemed both grotesque and amusing to whites."[20]

But what if dance is not essentially racial or even cultural? Hanna writes, "To dance is human, and humanity almost universally expresses itself in dance."[21] Why do some ascribe innate characteristics to entire people groups because they move their bodies in certain ways? Amazing, isn't it? It might be time to reevaluate our attitudes about how others dance—and how they live, for that matter. For now, let's rock and roll because nothing did more to break through the borders between white and Black dance culture than that music.

"We can't choose the music that life gives us, but
we can choose how to dance to it."

—UNKNOWN

I come from a musical family that was also a dancing one, at least on my mom's side. My mom often mentioned the different musical styles and dances of her youth. She talked about the vocal prowess of Paul Robeson and Bessie Smith, in addition to the elegance of Duke Ellington. And she was particularly fond of the musical genius Charlie Parker. (One aside, the latter was said to have been my first cousin twice removed.) Apparently, Mom loved his music but hated that his lifestyle included drugs. Moreover, there was a concern that I might emulate it. Turns out, I did briefly. This demonstrates how dance and music were frequently discussed in our home. And the broader point I am making is that music and dance hold an important place in many of our lives without us even realizing it.

---

18. Sachs, *World History*, 25.

19. Sachs, *World History,* 446.

20. Emery, *Black Dance*, 189.

21. Hanna, *To Dance Is Human*, 1.

That said, it was the names of the dances mentioned by my mom that fascinated me the most. And that was because she occasionally demonstrated them for me. I heard about the jitterbug, the black bottom, and the lindy hop, to name a few. She only alluded to some of the other dances because people thought they were obscene or vulgar. That is what I knew about the connection between dance and vulgarity. That is until I became aware of the national uproar over the gyrations of pop singer Elvis Presley. I could not have been more than six or seven years old, but I knew whatever he was doing was serious and seriously wrong.

What was Elvis's offense? He swiveled his hips "like a negro" when he sang. And that led to reactions such as this: "In the fall of 1956, Elvis Presley arrived, the music made a gradual transformation . . . dancing changed too."[22] Presley ruffled some feathers because "Hard-nosed executives reacted like frightened rabbits. After one debacle, the cameramen on the next show were ordered to photograph Elvis from the chest up only. It looked silly."[23] It took several years for the moral outrage over a white performer dancing like a negro to subside, but subside it did. Presley made it acceptable for white teenage fans to dance in this previously taboo manner. Soon teenage Jimi Calhoun provided the music white kids used for dancing. We played clubs, parties, dance halls, and fraternity parties all along the Northern California peninsula. Let me share how that started.

THE WUTZIT

A Roman Catholic priest named Walter E. Schmidt created a dance club inside the Santa Clara Youth Village called "Wutzit." The purpose of Wutzit was to provide a safe hangout for white teens. It was open Wednesday, Friday, and Saturday nights and had a dance floor, a stage, a game room, and a concession stand. There was a dress code and adult chaperones to ensure the dancing didn't get too hot and heavy. My bands played at dances there and we also entered "the battle of the bands." Rock and roll bands played two or three songs, and judges would evaluate the performances. Prizes were awarded to the bands achieving the highest score, much like what happens at an Olympic skating competition. Even the ancient Greeks had battles of the bands. Thomas Martin writes that one festival to honor the goddess Athena had "contests in music, dancing, poetry, and athletics."[24] But music is not what is important about Wutzit; race is.

22. Stearns and Stearns, *Jazz Dance*, 3.

23. Stearns and Stearns, *Jazz Dance*, 3.

24. Martin, *Ancient Greece*, 162.

My best friend in middle school was an Italian kid named Carl Fara-one. We became friends through competing against each other in basket-ball. Carl and I both lived on the east side of San Jose. It was somewhat multicultural, but the majority were Latinx. The Wutzit, located in Santa Clara, was an enclave of whiteness at that time. Even though several Black kids were in bands that played at Wutzit, I was the only one that I knew of to be a card-carrying member. That happened because Carl talked me into taking a bus to attend dances there, and I was adventurous enough to do it. So, once a week I would get on a city bus and ride for thirty minutes to attend dances populated entirely by white kids.

The Latinx kids danced at a place named the Hi Spot. These dances hap-pened in the basement of a YWCA building a few blocks east of the dividing line between white and darker-skinned people. It became the perfect place to see the beauty in the first-generation immigrant culture from south of the California border. Black kids never had a teen club of their own, though. That was either due to a lack of economic resources or because we were small in number. It didn't matter why because we sure danced to our heart's content in private homes. However, the ethnic makeup of teen clubs is not the topic at hand. It is the types of dances the kids were doing that matters.

The same songs were popular with all three groups, yet the kids who attended each separate club created different dances in response. To fast songs, the white kids danced the stroll and the bop. But the Latinx and Af-rican American kids did the Texas hop. When the DJ played slow songs, the white kids danced differently to them too. Black kids held their partners very close, almost hugging, and engaged in a rolling motion as they danced. The white kids didn't get too close to their partners, and their style had more swing. There was even a slow dance called the Wutzit. There was no "rolling" allowed at Wutzit. In fact, part of the chaperone's job was to monitor how close you held your partner.

Here's what a friend named Ron posted about the Wutzit dance on Facebook: "Not too close, Father Schmidt with his flashlight." What is that about? Well, Father Schmidt patrolled the dance floor with a flashlight to monitor how close you danced. The expectation was the chaperone should be able to see light between the dancing bodies. A warning tap on the shoul-der followed if a couple got too close. That gives you an idea of the differ-ence between Black and white slow dancing. The fact that yesterday's teens danced differently to the same songs along "racial lines" could be a meta-phor for how we still see Black and white social interaction today. Border walls of this type demonstrate that there should not be two ways of doing the same thing. The fact these distinctions in dance styles evaporated over time offers hope.

ROCK-A-TEENS

The Rock-A-Teens was the name of the first band that paid me to perform. The players were Clark Baldwin, Franz Beelard, Skip Spence, Ted and Gary Waltrip, and Danny Leon, all of whom were white. And then there was me, the only Black kid in the band. Outside of my bus excursions to Wutzit my knowledge of San Jose was pretty much limited to the ethnic east side. When I began playing music at the white teen clubs in the upscale areas of the Santa Clara Valley, such as Saratoga, Campbell, and Los Gatos, it affected me profoundly. Until then, I had no idea I lived on "that side of town." Please realize there were never any kids that looked like me in those places. Over time music and dance provided a bridge to acceptance and making genuine friends.

THE TIKI

The Tiki was a teen "nightclub" open on weekends during daylight hours. I first picked up a bass guitar there. Now meet Chubby Checker. Jim Ryan writes, "While Elvis Presley made dancing a controversial part of the rock and roll experience . . . Checker took the popularity of dancing to a new level as 'The Twist' sparked a U.S. dance craze."[25] And twist away is precisely what all the kids, Black, brown, and white did at the Tiki. The Beatles made the late 1960s an exciting time for everyone. But what excited me was that it was the first time I saw whites and Blacks doing the same dance to the same music.

Despite that, something called colorism entered the picture. Simply put, colorism is a preference for the lighter skin tone. It began to blur the gains Martin Luther King's dream of integration had made. How? According to a *Time* magazine article, "A person's skin color is an irrefutable visual fact that is impossible to hide, whereas race is a constructed, quasi-scientific classification that is often only visible on a government form."[26] As a result, the darker hues were denigrated through colorism. This shows how it affected people.

Hank Ballard, a Black singer, wrote the song "The Twist." How the white record-buying public received it is an example of colorism. Initially, white kids dismissed that song without so much as a hearing. But they enthusiastically accepted a version of it by the lighter-skinned Chubby Checker. Industry charts rank records using sales figures and media reports. The

25. Ryan, "Chubby Checker Looks Back," line 10.
26. Tharps, "Difference Between Racism and Colorism," line 11.

performance by the darker-skinned Ballard charted at number twenty-eight on the primarily white pop charts. And it reached number six on the soul or African American charts. However, the version by the lighter-skinned Checker was a smashing success. That record went on to achieve a higher position on both charts. It became the only single recording to chart number one twice on the much more lucrative pop charts.

The disparity in success happened when it was common for white musical artists to "cover," meaning rerecord, a song by a Black entertainer. White musicians would then have a much bigger hit with it. Record promoters and record buyers assumed that white kids should dance to music made by white musicians. A myth circulated that Black music could permanently damage white kids. There were even journalists covering the British blues renaissance of the 1960s who were surprised that white English kids would be interested in Black music from the American Delta.

The good people of New Orleans distributed a flyer around the city with the words "STOP" placed at the top in emboldened letters. It read, "If you don't want Negros in your home or business, call the radio station and ask them not to play their records."[27] The flyer explained that "the screaming, idiotic words and savage music of their [black] records are undermining the morals of our white American youth."[28]

Amazingly, these "facts" seeped into popular culture without anyone identifying any negative consequences tied to white people's exposure to Black music. Groundless race theories like that have ruined way too many lives. Unfortunately, we have dismissed some of them only to replace them with others equally as perplexing. Most of us have heard "rap crap" or "thug music" roll off people's lips about hip-hop, haven't we? Whether one intends to or not, using those phrases sends the same message as the ad I just quoted.

THE SWIM

My music career's rise from playing teen clubs to major venues resulted from another song that became a dance craze. That was a song named "C'mon and Swim," performed by Bobby Freeman, whom I backed at the ripe old age of fifteen and a half. However, music is not my reason for mentioning this; the dance is. Black funk superstar Sly Stone wrote the song. It became a fixture in white America. The dance became the dance of dances for people immersed in surf culture. Scores of surf films and James Bond movies used it. The dance's objective was to mimic a swimmer's arm movements while

27. nmaahc.si.edu, "Handbill."
28. nmaahc.si.edu, "Handbill."

standing erect and wiggling the hips. Some would even hold their noses and lower their shoulders like doing a deep water dive. The dance was light-hearted and silly, which led to many smiles as the kids danced.

There is another reason why I included the swim in this conversation. When the Beatles became unimaginably popular, thousands of kids bought guitars. They grew their hair long, hoping to become the next big thing. If you looked English or had an English accent, that brought the chances of success even closer. A guy in New Zealand named Ray Columbus recorded a version of the swim a year after Freeman's. It was a major hit in his native country. Following his success in New Zealand, Ray decided to do his take on what was called the British Invasion and conquer America himself.

Guess who he ran into upon arriving in San Francisco? Me and Clark from The Rock-A-Teens, with whom I had also played in Bobby Freeman's band. The two of us would put a band together to back Columbus. Seren-dipitous as that may seem, what is important here is how a dance crossed a national border, and an ocean in the process. Just think, the swim was able to reach across sixty-five hundred miles and join a shaggy haired New Zealand pop singer with two California soul and funk musicians. The twist, the swim, and several other dances with names from the animal world, like the duck, the dog, and the pony, marked the rise of America's full-blown dance renaissance. What was to come next?

GO-GO DANCERS

By the middle 1960s, dancing had become ubiquitous at young adult hang-outs. Almost every young adult was dancing. So what should an enterprising nightclub owner do to increase profit? Provide an option for nondancing customers to watch both people dance on the floor and beautiful "go-go" dancers in cages. It worked. The go-go dance craze became the next fad to sweep America's rock and roll nightclub circuit. Establishments such as the Whisky A Go Go in Hollywood, the Pussy-Cat A Go Go in Las Vegas, and hundreds of spin-offs had women in cages elevated above their bandstands dancing to our music in three- to four-song shifts. You can believe they were in excellent physical condition after a few weeks of gyrating to up-tempo rock and roll beats.

Go-go dancing extended beyond nightclubs too. Go-go dancers soon accompanied rock bands on television programs such as *Hullabaloo* and *Where the Action Is*, and in many major films. However, when Carol Doda began go-go dancing topless at a club named The Condor in San Fran-cisco, she became the most famous go-go dancer in the world. Ironically, to start her show, she danced the swim on top of a grand piano lowered from the ceiling. That was a sight, all right! The Condor was right next door to a club named Big Al's. My brother worked there, and it is close to where I played before we took our own go-go show on the road to Alaska. That story is next.

Topless bars were the next logical step from costumed women dancing in rock's version of a gilded cage. At least, that seemed logical to many nightclub owners desiring additional revenue streams. Some unsavory characters ran many nightclubs where the topless women danced, to put it mildly. Jimmy Sumpter was one of those owners. He owned the club where my brother and I performed, named the Idle Hour Supper Club, in Anchorage, Alaska. The Idle Hour had gained notoriety for having Christine Jorgenson, "who captured international headlines . . . as the first person in the United States to undergo a successful gender-reassignment operation,"[29] perform a few years before our band arrived.

This is what was written about our boss: "In those years, Sumpter owned and operated . . . topless/strip clubs including The Kit Kat and The Sportsman Too. He was a colorful character and on the periphery of—if not directly involved in—a couple of homicides."[30] True crime writer Mike Gordon penned a story that illustrates the temperament of my former boss. He writes, "Jimmy put a reward on the street of $10,000 cash for information about the murderer of his family, but rumor had it that it was for anyone killing a member of the gang, so it might be assumed that the gang got rid of Ziegler [the prime suspect] themselves in order to pacify Jimmy Sumpter."[31] Can you imagine what it was like to see these types of characters when you showed up for work every day?

ANGELS OR JOKERS

Alaska was not the only place where I had to worry about gangs. Once back in the San Francisco Bay area, I joined a different band and began playing the club circuit there. One of those was a nightclub named the Adriatic, in San Jose. It was not populated by go-go dancers, bare-chested women, or even mobsters—it was frequented by the notorious motorcycle gang the Hells Angels. Every night Carol Stallings, our lead vocalist, would sing a Beatles song with a lyric that contained the word "joker" in it. At the time there was another biker gang in the area named the Gypsy Jokers. They were

29. Britannica.com, "Christine Jorgenson."
30. Haines, "Idle Hour," para. 8, line 3.
31. Gordon, "Hired Gun," para. 5, line 7.

the Hells Angels' archrivals and the two did not get along. One night after performing that particular song, I was told that hearing us sing "joker" did not sit well with the Angels.

There are just some people who do not wish their enemies to be thought of highly. They would prefer their enemies to be viewed with the same amount of contempt that they have for them. In light of that, I asked Carol to change the word "joker" to "angel." At the risk of oversimplification, intentionally developing contempt for the other is how many handle politics, Black/white race relations, and religion, isn't it? The song Carol sang was named "Come Together." The irony is the song's lyrics pleaded for people in conflict to "come together right now." Those are words we need to pay attention to today. Living them out would be even better.

BORDER DANCING

The authors of *Moving History/Dancing Cultures* write, "Every dance reveals its own aesthetic and moorings within its basic movement vocabulary."[32] That says it is possible to tell what something is by how it moves. There is a traditional Israeli dance named the hora. It is "performed at Jewish weddings where the newlyweds are lifted into the air while their family and friends dance in circles around them."[33] However, the types of lines you find in much of American folk dance are straight. Dancing in a straight line can guide a person's foot placement. That happens in the line dance enjoyed by country music lovers. But line dancing is negatively impacted if someone steps out of line.

Line dancers understand they must conform to a set pattern to keep things going smoothly. Interestingly, something else happens when circular lines are danced, as in our Jewish example. The circle gives you more flexibility. In this type of dance, you can focus on the dancers across and beside you. It is tough to step out of line when dancing in a circle. However, when circles are formed, even in dance, take care to ensure they don't become borders of exclusion. Instead, make this your prayer: "Lead us into the circle dance of justice, into the wondrous dances of peace. Turn our hopes of peace and peaceful transitions into the joyous dance of celebration."[34]

There is a Greek word with a similar sound to the hora dance. It is spelled similarly, horos, but has an entirely different meaning. What I find interesting, and hopefully not getting too technical, is that in New

32. Dils and Albright, *Moving History/Dancing Cultures*, 95.

33. Kreuger, "What to Know About the Jewish Hora Dance," line 6.

34. Worldinprayer.org, "World News This Week in Prayer," para. 7.

Testament Greek, the word *horos* is defined this way, "From the noun . . . (*horos*), meaning boundary."[35] Yet, when you Google the same word you can find this definition: "Horos, khoros, choros . . . means 'dance' in the Greek language."[36] This word occurs in the names of numerous Greek dances like the Tapeinos horos.

Those two definitions serve as the basis for the concept of border dance. It is also one of the reasons for this book's title. At this point, I would ask you to think about how many people in your immediate circle of friends, meaning those closest to you, have a skin color different from yours. If there are none, are you willing to cross a border to make some? Improved race relations result from intimacy, just like dancing with a person you love. Let's dance!

35. Abarim-publications.com, "Horos."
36. Definitions.net, "Horos."

SECTION ONE

Nationalism

"Our true nationality is mankind."
—H. G. WELLS

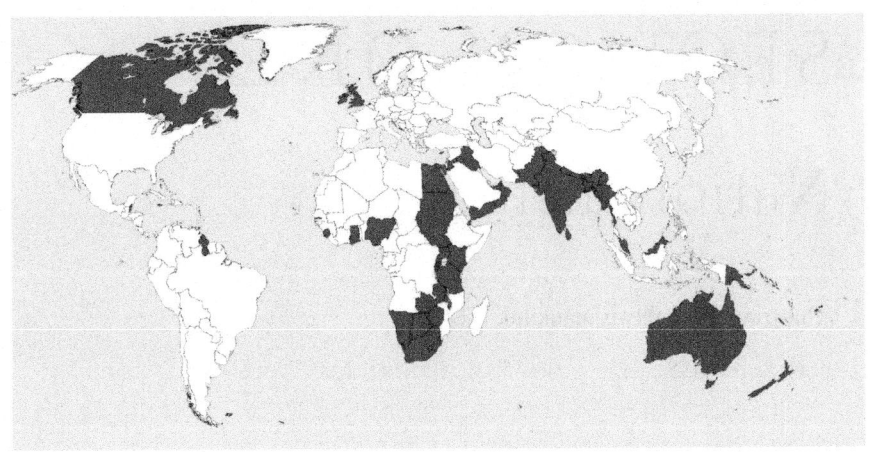

The British Empire in the 1920s

CHAPTER 2, PART ONE

The West

For God and the Empire

IT ALL STARTED HERE

WORLD HISTORY AS WE presently know it was forged in the crucible of Western conquest. As Brian Bantum notes, "The presence of Europe among the peoples of the world was not mere political or economic expediency: it served to recreate the world."[1] Western powers seized control of most of the earth's landmass at different times all under the pretext of spreading civilization and, secondarily, Christianity. Part of that process led to the subjugation of many Indigenous people. One group in particular had a success rate that outdistanced the rest, the British. At its peak in the 1920s, the British Empire was the largest in history. Estimates are that it ruled over at least 400 million people. That would have been about 25 percent of the world population. And as pictured on the map, the empire covered about 24 percent of the earth's surface. I am suggesting that the salient features of modern world history begin here, at the formation of the British Empire.

Jared Diamond authored *Guns, Germs, and Steel*, for which he won a Pulitzer Prize. The book focuses on world history presented in a non-traditional format. In it, Diamond offers reasons why human populations have different survival rates. I found one question in the book relevant to this section's premise. "What significance, if any, do the continent's differing

---

1. Bantum, *Redeeming Mulatto*, 15.

dates of settlement have for subsequent history?"[2] Diamond suggests that a timeline of human progress exists, and knowing it helps to explain the present. That may be true, but perhaps we should ask, "Who settled what, and who gave whom the right to do so?" The logical follow-up to that question would be, "And who did what to whom to achieve it?"

Now let us go back to where it all began. That is because with conquest comes cultural absorption, and part of what was absorbed was dance. A word of caution is needed here. What you are about to read is about more than dance. But by using dance as an exemplar, I am attempting to illustrate how much we are influenced by the corrosive ideology of race. And that racial ideas permeate something so fundamentally innocent as dance. British dance, including the Irish and Scottish varieties, are types of folk dance. But who will you dance with if you are confused about who qualifies as "your folk"?

I just mentioned confusion. Think about this. There is a great deal of human variation, so it can be challenging to identify the group one should call "my folk." Let us use the history of the island where England is located to illustrate the point. Numerous historians have written that English history is one of invasion by tribes with names such as Angles, Celts, Gauls, Gaels, Romans, Danes, Normans, Norsemen, and so on. Let us suppose that each of those tribes brought a distinct culture to the island. With a mix like that, how can we be sure which of these sources spawned the majority of today's English people?

For centuries there was not one England. Several "mini" kingdoms occupied much of the land. A state of anxiety existed on the island because people were always preparing for the next war. Over time, a blending process occurred and they merged into four larger kingdoms: East Anglia, Mercia, Wessex, and Northumbria. At a later date, England became one. That set the stage for the emergence of the "British race." This is the one that former prime minister Winston Churchill believed to be "the best in the world."[3] We will hear more from him later.

How did all of these disparate groups come to function as one nation-state? They devised a system of titles to indicate a person's status in society. David Cannadine writes that the British believed their society was "providentially ordained, hierarchically ordered and organically inter-connected."[4] He lists "monarchs, aristocrats, courtiers, heralds, lawyers, clergy and scholars"[5]

---

2. Diamond, *Guns, Germs, and Steel*, 50.

3. Toye, *Churchill's Empire*, 18.

4. Cannadine, *Rise and Fall*, 26.

5. Cannadine, *Rise and Fall*, 27.

as being the movers and shakers. Social differences were perceived vertically using a bottom-to-top concept in the same way many view racial groupings today. There were others who would be described as "working class" as well. Several famous English blues musicians from my bass-playing years fit that mold. A working-class background in England sounds like mine as a person of African descent living in the US. The way to describe life in that environment is by using one word, *rough*.

Early on, English people would refer to outsiders as races. However, they managed to do so without basing it on skin color, which amounts to not much more than a dermatological issue. Think through the following description. Local observers referred to the tribes invading England as "pagan races." We define a pagan as a person who holds religious views that are not in step with the mainstream. Taken together, this expresses how many view the religiously and racially different today, out of step.

In contrast to a pagan, most religious people in Britain understood their station in life. They also knew what responsibilities came with it. According to Cannadine, people were expected "to honor and obey the King . . . to order myself lowly and reverently to all my betters . . . to do my duty in the state of life which it shall please God to call me."[6] Living out each item on the list was viewed as a sacred responsibility. We will deal with the notion that inequality is a "calling of God" in a later section. For now, it is worth mentioning that the dance styles of every class influenced English folk dance. And this amalgam further demonstrates how dance brings people together. In addition to being a means of connecting people, dance also functions as a bonding agent. This occurs even when dancers do not have much in common. Discouragingly, this does not happen with all people. Journalist Sanjoy Roy describes how some people's lives were affected differently.

> "Like Britain itself," says dance history professor Ramsay Burt, "British dance has been informed by different waves of immigration." Well, that is a truism: ballet took root through the determination of a Polish woman, Marie Rambert, and an Irishwoman, Ninette de Valois, and modern dance was seeded by exiles from Germany in the 1930s and visitors from America in the 50s and 60s. But those stories are not what Burt is getting at. What about black people's stories?[7]

6. Cannadine, *Rise and Fall*, 27.

7. Roy, "How black dancers brought a new dynamism to British dance," para. 1.

Julie Felix

Let us check out a few of those Black dancers' stories, beginning with a woman named Julie Felix. Recently I watched a documentary about her. She was the first Black ballerina to gain national recognition in Britain. In one interview, she spoke of her dedication to ballet from her earliest memories. Julie told the interviewer that her mom couldn't believe that she danced everywhere. Around the house, in the park, and even at school, Julie danced. Julie would later train at Rambert ballet school. There she was offered a professional contract by a highly respected dance company.

However, the company's brain trust withdrew that chance of a lifetime opportunity. The reason? They decided her brown skin would be difficult to blend into a line of dancers featuring white swans. Julie would later say, "I had never thought of the refined world of ballet as being what we might now describe as institutionally racist . . . because I didn't experience any racial issues or difficulties before that. I didn't think there was anything wrong with the color of my skin. I thought that I was talented and that would be enough."[8]

People who believe that merit determines a person's success in life tend to downplay examples of this type. In doing so, they deny the stranglehold race has on everyday life. The reason is that racism is self-evident to those who have been affected by it. In contrast, racism is invisible to those who haven't experienced it. They see an equal playing field and miss the racialized gopher holes that cause many a player to trip. Sadly, Julie would soon face racism in the USA as well. That included "a frightening confrontation with the Ku Klux Klan—but the highs outweighed the lows; Julie danced alongside Lionel Richie at the LA Olympics and her performances were watched by the world's biggest stars including Michael Jackson and Prince."[9]

It is crucial to keep in mind that her KKK encounter is a relatively recent event. I can relate because early in my music career, I experienced similar treatment while touring England. For me, her story seems like a recurring nightmare that spans time and international borders. Despite the alarming frequency of such events, some will never acknowledge they even happen. But as British author David Olusoga laments, "Almost every black or mixed-race person of my generation has a story of racial violence to tell . . . these stories range from humiliation to hospitalization."[10] Olusoga explains that these stories are "rarely shared beyond family circles."[11]

8. Rose, "Julie Felix," para. 4.

9. Trewhela, "Britain's First Black Ballerina," para. 4

10. Olusoga, *Black and British*, xvii.

11. Olusoga, *Black and British*, xvii.

Why hide them? Because when confronted with these issues, the majority culture develops alternative explanations. To paraphrase journalist Krista Tippett, you can disagree with people's opinions, but you shouldn't doubt their experiences. Unfortunately, questioning Black people's stories has been a convenient way to avoid facing the harsh reality of racism. But the realities of racism cannot be understood from the sidelines, only by living them. These stories are important. However, if not heard, they will do nothing to ease racial tensions.

Berto Pasuka and Richie Riley

Berto Pasuka and Richie Riley cofounded Les Ballets Nègres, the first Black ballet company in Europe. After overcoming long odds, they established a dance troupe. The production company "choreographed ballets that dealt with African/Caribbean traditions and Black/white relationships . . . The company was comprised of dancers from the West Indies, West Africa, England, and the U.S."[12] Notice that the dancers of African descent came from different geographies and cultures. But regardless of their countries of origin, they were viewed as "Black."

The white dancing community's limited perception of Black people affected how Pasuka and Riley decided on a name for their dance troupe. They considered using the word *black* in the name, but they knew it had nothing but negative connotations. They also knew that in the West, the adjective *black* stigmatizes and diminishes the value of the noun it modifies. For example, history's most deadly pandemic was dubbed the Black Death. And an illegal or inferior product is sold on a black market. Even progressive Hollywood has a "blacklist" for actors and films it rejects.

Pasuka and Riley also decided against using the word *colored*. They thought it may imply that a "normal" skin tone exists but just got "painted over." This means African skin becomes black the same way children color pictures with crayons. So they settled on a name that used the French spelling of the word negro, *Negres*. This was done to avoid being confused with how Black people were labeled in America. Richard Jenkins exposes the need for that, writing, "Social groups [which a dance troupe is] define themselves . . . Social categories [such as races] are identified, defined and delineated by others."[13]

In a bit of irony, Black people ran away from being called "colored," only to run right into "person of color." That is a problem, right? However,

12. Les Ballets Nègres scrapbook, para. 1.

13. Jenkins, *Rethinking Ethnicity*, 55.

it might be possible to combine the two as convicted killer Roddy Bryan did. He described his victim, Ahmaud Arbery, as "the colored black guy." That did not happen in 1950. This guy said those words in 2020. You will re-encounter Roddy shortly.

The fact that two pioneers had so many things to consider before the dancing even began saddens me. Their problems stemmed from a different type of color blindness. There was a disregard for the legitimacy and dignity of Black culture. As Sarah Derbew notes, "Geopolitical renderings of blackness . . . with no regard for historical context promote neocolonial narratives."[14] These narratives suggest darker-skinned people are in need of some form of outside control to prosper. Many people just accept these narratives at face value. When that happens, they become the "facts" used as a basis for all types of cruelty. When the issue is race, truth becomes everything! And if Black people continue to be defined by the perceptions of the Western eye, where does that land?

However, maybe it doesn't matter what is perceived about race if the root of the presumptions is fear. Fear causes people to act irrationally. Controlling emotions is critical because fear distorts its object. Former boxing champion Mike Tyson won many fights before they even started. That happened because his menacing and intimidating aura had many opponents shaking in their boots before the first bell had even rung. His opponents were slow to realize that Tyson was just another boxer. And despite his enormous skill, his punches were just punches. Similarly, a perception of race rooted in fear causes Black skin to appear ominous instead of being what it is, just skin.

Elroy Josephs

I would like to introduce you to Elroy Josephs. His career encapsulates everything that we have been discussing. Josephs migrated from Jamaica to Britain. Upon arrival he became a professional dancer and entrepreneur. He also became the first Black dancer to teach at a British university. Let me be as clear as I can be. We are discussing dance and race's impact on this art form. Black and white relations related to the disparity of power are political equations. But Black and white relations related to dance, equality, and human dignity are sociological concerns. Then it becomes a matter for the British people, not politicians, to sort out. In my view, those are separate concerns. Let us look at some of the things written about Josephs by the respected dance historian Ramsey Burt.

14. Derbew, "Blackness in Antiquity," para. 7.

Elroy Josephs claimed that the wonderful tradition of black British dancing should be recognized for what it is and duly celebrated. In the second decade of the twenty-first century, many black British dancers are still waiting for this, while the rise of a xenophobic populist nationalism in Britain and other European countries means that questions about how to negotiate identities in inclusive ways are more pertinent than ever.[15]

Burt illustrates the vision and the passion of the man by writing, "Josephs was moving from a Caribbean society where social hierarchy was grounded in graduated shades of Blackness to a country where these shades of difference were no longer socially distinguishable, but there was a sharp and often brutal distinction between black and white"[16] in Britain. That distinction would significantly affect how Josephs's entrepreneurial efforts were received. And also how successful they would be.

Josephs obtained "funds from the Arts Council . . . the trust had provided summer schools in which international teachers of neo-traditional African and Caribbean dance and drumming taught classes to the young black British dancers."[17] Several people objected to the dances being too African and not enough British. With that came the end of the funding. Sadly, racial bias put the brakes on an entrepreneurial enterprise. If you cannot see the problem, maybe this analogy will help. Imagine a grant is given to a person from the Netherlands to open a bakery. Now imagine the funds are withdrawn because the pastries are too Dutch. Similarly, the problem wasn't the dances, but rather the color of the dancers' skin.

Conflicts arise when people feel others aren't "like us" enough to be "with us." Truthfully, I have had similar thoughts about fellow musicians who dressed differently than the people in my band. I have also thought the same thing about other people who worship Christ differently than I do. Yet in this case, white aversion to African influence on popular dance ends with the marginalization of the people involved. Later, we will see how African influence in dance resulted in restrictions inside white churches. But for now, let's draw a contrast between British and American dance. You will better understand why this chapter is titled "it all started here" after reading what comes next.

15. Burt, "Elroy Josephs and the Hidden Costs," para. 26.
16. Burt, "Elroy Josephs and the Hidden Costs," para. 13.
17. Burt, "Elroy Josephs," para. 1.

BRITISH INSPIRATION

We have been discussing Black ballet practitioners in Britain, and the authors of *Jazz Dance* quote Dame Ninette de Valois, of the Royal Ballet of England, as having said, "All Ballets' fundamental steps . . . are derived from the folk dance of Western Europe."[18] They then offer us this perspective germane to our topic: "Indeed all dance may be said to derive ultimately from the folk."[19] This short but powerful statement proves how important it is to review the British people's makeup and influence before discussing specific dance styles. Additionally, it is incredible that stories about professional dancers shadow this chapter's basic premise that it all started here.

The "it" I am referring to is the ability of dance to transcend every imaginable border as no other art form has done. Dance "is the most personal of all the arts . . . It is the oldest for this very reason, and it is the newest because it springs from the very breath of life."[20] There is a colloquialism that is quite popular today and that is "new-old." The meaning is as it sounds. My childhood friend named his band Lenny Goldsmith and the New-Old. That is because they perform the music he and I played decades ago, along with his more recent original compositions. New-old can describe many things: a band, a restored classic car, a specialty guitar called "a relic," and America! The US is a new-old version of Britain in many areas of our culture. That includes dance and that is my point.

It is also true that the America that exists today is markedly different from the Britain of the past. However, American culture has always been derivative of English culture. That has been true no matter what political rhetoric was employed to obscure the fact. As with the class-based hierarchies of medieval England, Americans have always perceived that there can be unity in diversity. They believe it can work as long as everyone stays in their own lane. The lane analogy might have been valid had the lanes been of equal size and quality. But it breaks down when you consider those lanes have never been either for outside groups.

18. Stearns and Stearns, *Jazz Dance*, xvi.
19. Stearns and Stearns, *Jazz Dance*, xvi.
20. Terry, *Invitation to Dance*, 16.

CHAPTER 2, PART TWO

Freedom Jazz Dance

Now, LET US TURN our attention to a uniquely American art form called "jazz dance." This dance has "evolved along parallels to jazz music."[1] As we talk about jazz music, I want to point out a few things. There is a song titled "The Freedom Jazz Dance" that the trumpeter Miles Davis popularized and that I performed with several bands. Although the song is free-form jazz, the rhythm allows a person to dance to it. That song is a challenge to play. That is because its complex melodies are supported by danceable rhythms. Pianist Ron Drotos noted that the song "is a jazz-rock piece that was composed by tenor saxophonist Eddie Harris . . . The "free" in the title comes from the fact that there's only one chord, a Bb7, and during your solos you can play anything you like over it."[2]

It is certainly accurate to describe jazz's impact as liberating. However, jazz dance is equally freeing. That is because free-form dance allows a person to use their body to metaphorically "play all over" the dance floor any way they choose. There was a band called Sun Ra Arkestra that exemplified free-form music and dance. Writer John Sinclair said, "First of all, it would be about anywhere between 12 and 20 people in the Arkestra. And each would be costumed in a unique garb. Colorful. African-influenced. Space-influenced."[3] Dancers in front of the band would interpret the abstract music using their own freestyle dance. Watching Sun Ra's dancers

---

1. Stearns and Stearns, *Jazz Dance.* xvi.
2. Dotros, "Freedom Jazz Dance," line 1.
3. Farberman, "Why Is Sun Ra Finally Having His Moment?," para. 6.

mesmerize an audience is proof that dance expresses every emotion human beings experience. To illustrate my point, I will break down the three words in the song's title, *freedom, jazz,* and *dance.*

FREEDOM

America's political promise of liberty and justice was great news to one specific group of people. However, when the founders did not distribute rights equally, it caused nightmares for others. Freedom and equality were said to be the goals of the American revolution. But many of the revolutionaries owned enslaved Africans while they were fighting for their brand of freedom. Using that backlight to improve visibility, what does freedom look like anyway? Arthur Mitchell, the first Black dancer with the New York City Ballet, gives us a hint through analogy. He rhetorically asks, "What does dance give you? The freedom to be who you are and do what you want to do."[4]

If only that were true of what American independence from England brought people of African descent. Rather than a dance partner in the American dream, some continue to see Black people as an obstacle to it. That distrust prevents Black people from "being who they want to be" and "doing what they want to do." When people dance, they "begin to recognize one another as friend . . . by their dancing styles,"[5] writes Kimerer Lamothe. And by observing the dance styles of others, "they recognize themselves."[6] Do you think many white people can see themselves in a Black person?

And what if "who you are" was decided for you by a group of people you had never met long before you took up dancing? Ironically the word *Black* has been used for African people the same way the British used royal titles. They used *Princess, Duke, Lord,* etc., to stratify. And today we use "racial titles" to accomplish the same end. But hierarchical social constructs, and rigid musical patterns with fixed positions, are the opposite of true freedom. And those concepts are also in contradiction to the next word in the title of the song.

4. Mitchell, "What Does Dance Give You?"

5. Lamothe, *Why We Dance,* 192.

6. Lamothe, *Why We Dance,* 192.

JAZZ

A master jazz musician said to a young player, "It is [jazz] not magic, but it should seem that it is."[7] Seeing music this way broadens the horizons of an aspiring musician. And good jazz should leave both listener and player in a state of utter amazement. The fact that one instrumentalist can pull endless amounts of musical phrases out of what seems to be nowhere is impressive. At times it can sound like jazz musicians are "playing anything." But the reality is they are playing everything that is appropriate. It takes hours upon hours of practice for a jazz player to be physically agile enough to pull off that "magic." For a new musical phrase to flow, the mind must be crammed full of scales and melodies from the past. Playing jazz takes an enormous amount of dedication and hard work. If you think about it, so does loving others in the way Jesus would have us.

However, the parallel does not end there. You must also look for new and better ways to express that love. Jazz music does not have much value if it can't be heard. Love does not have much value if it can't be felt. Please keep the following in mind as you make your way through this book. Many of the enslavers identified as Christian, and brutality is how they supposedly showed Christ's love. Jazz musicians practice scales on their instruments. It is a Christian's responsibility to practice love in the lives of others. Do you believe it is a Christian virtue to use violence to control others? Sadly, many people would answer yes if they think it will keep them safe.

DANCE (DARKLY)

Lynn Fauley Emery writes of a process called "dancing the slaves" while transporting them away from their homeland. She quotes a British enslaver as writing in 1694, "We . . . would let the slaves come up into the sun and air themselves, and make them jump and dance for an hour or two to our bag-pipes, harp, and fiddle."[8] That sounds like fun, right? Seriously? Fun, but for whom? The crew's job was to keep them dancing, "but it was only done by a frequent use of the cat."[9] A cat was "a whip that was woven and flowed into nine separate pieces . . . each piece had a knot in the middle, and broken glass, and nails at the very end."[10] The pain must have been unbearable.

---

7. Crouch, *Kansas City Lightening*, 177.

8. Emery, *Black Dance*, 9.

9. Emery, *Black Dance*, 6.

10. Sibley, "Whipping," para. 3.

The living conditions for enslaved people aboard slave ships were abysmal. Although they danced, it was in an environment of utter cruelty. To maximize profit, ships designed to carry one hundred passengers were stuffed with three to four times that many captive Africans. The soon-to-be enslaved people were chained together. Enslavers stacked them on top of each other to fit as many as possible in the cargo holds. And they stayed that way for up to three months!

The enslavers' behavior sounds morally deficient, not commercially efficient, to me. A shameful act like that "gives thought to the ironic way of how white slave masters saw the slaves as savages, and yet dispensed such 'savage' punishment to the slaves by whipping them unmercifully, even while allowing others to watch."[11] It seems violence directed at Black skin is an age-old practice in the West. Sadly, it remains so. One of the methods used by the enslavers to procure their "cargo" was to take advantage of the African's love of dance.

Emery quotes an elderly ex-enslaved person named Thomas Johns. When interviewed in the 1930s, Johns lived in the state of Texas. He said his father had been born in Africa before being stolen and brought to Savannah, Georgia. Johns told one story about how dance was used in the kidnapping. He said, "De way dey was stole, dey was asked to dance on a ship which some white men had, and my aunt said it was early in de next mornin' when dey away from land and all dey could see was de water all 'round."[12] It was at that point they realized they no longer had a home.

That must have been horrifying. Imagine what it would be like to attend a party on a friend's yacht. The following day you wake up chained to people you don't know and who speak a different language. But you and everyone else share this one thing. Life as you have known it is over! My point is that dance appears in the oddest places, including amid criminal behavior. And there really is no other way to characterize the shenanigans of the enslavers except criminal.

Dance was used in other cruel ways on the voyage between Africa and the West. The purveyors of human flesh would force the enslaved to dance for no other purpose than to entertain themselves. Occasionally, they would force their captives to dance for hours on end to punish them for "misbehaving." Considering their limited amount of mobility, what could they do that was so bad? But even in situations like this, dance might have been a faint reminder of the lives they left behind. Dance might have even had a soothing effect on their troubled souls. It is ironic that those

11. Sibley, "Whipping," para. 3.
12. Emery, *Black Dance,* 3.

who used dance to show their power over African bodies, could have unwittingly produced something positive for their helpless and hopeless captives.

MEMBERS OF ONE ANOTHER

All of this demonstrates that like the dance the swim, dance moves across oceans easily. Unfortunately, so do the biases and prejudices that divide. There is a problem with that. To understand why, let's turn to the definition of *kinfolk*. That word has the root *kin*, which is "from Old English *cynn*, "family; race; kind."[13] Notice that this word encompasses three social groupings where much of our conflict occurs. The idea of kinship is summarized in the preamble to the United States Constitution. It reads, "We the people!" Is the word "we" a cliché? Should the word "we" refer to a subset the way the Danes or Celts were categorized in England? Or should the word refer to a cross section of "kins" for everyone to socialize with, trust, and love. Definitely! So let us make "we" mean something. Here is how.

Musician Stephen Stills recorded a song titled "Change Partners." The storyline is about a yearly event the uber-rich organize called a debutante ball. These balls are rites of passage for young women entering high society. The balls' activities consist of a lavish meal, speeches, and dancing. The young debutantes dance with several partners in order to interact with as many single men as possible. Perhaps that is why the songwriter used the ball as a reference point. But changing partners is also a metaphor for life. We know change will enter all of our lives. We also know when change happens, we learn to adjust to it. But for some reason when it comes to race, many still feel hesitant to change partners. These people prefer to dance the same way and with the same people.

Allow me to stretch the ball metaphor a little further. At every party some people refuse to dance and they are called wallflowers. A wallflower is someone who attends a party and once there, will not interact with others. That is how racism continues. Way too many people stand by and refuse to take part in bringing it to an end. It is worth remembering that whether a wallflower dances or not, they did receive an invitation.

When was the last time you intentionally invited someone of a different race to something? Maybe this is a better question. If you were planning a dinner in your home, do you know any people from another race well enough to invite? The rock band Traffic recorded a song asking

13. Etymonline.com, "Kin."

people to do a dance that everyone could join in. It all starts with you if that dance is ever going to happen! Next, we discuss how some Western powers stepped on people's toes in the Southern Hemisphere with their overly aggressive dances.

CHAPTER 3, PART ONE

The Southern Hemisphere

"I do not want to miss a good chance of getting us a
slice of this magnificent African cake."[1]

—Leopold II

AFRICA

IN 1898 BRITISH PRIME minister Lord Salisbury said, "The nations of the
earth are divided into the sheep and the wolves—the fat and defenseless
against the hungry and strong."[2] Now fold in this additional comment,
"Countries like Italy, Flanders and India were 'soft,' 'meek' and 'effeminate,'
there to be invaded by stronger powers."[3] That reflects the mindset many
Western politicians had that caused two world wars where several millions
of lives were lost. They viewed the world as being what one author called "a
playground for the strong."[4]

But if the stronger will inevitably defeat the weaker, why didn't the
dinosaurs survive? They were stronger than fruit flies, but fruit flies have
survived 200 million years. There is also the possibility of considering
cockroaches. After all, they have survived for 300 million years despite the

1. Goodreads.com, "Leopold II."
2. Vaguelyinteresting.co.uk, "Dying nations of the world," para. 6.
3. Vaguelyinteresting.co.uk, "Dying nations of the world," para. 6.
4. Holland, *Dominion*, 154.

strength and ingenuity of those intent on destroying them. Humor aside, using Darwin's survival of the fittest to explain why some people trample on the rights of others is not very satisfying. That is because it evades the ethical question.

The power politics of entitlement have had a devastating effect on the global South. That is sad because the majority of the world's Christians live there. For this book the global South includes Africa, South America, Australia, and to some extent, India, at least politically. That is because once India and Africa were absorbed into the British Empire, their fates became intertwined. As a result, many thousands of Indians were forcibly relocated to British colonies in Africa and South America. You will soon see that geographically and historically, India belongs in the East. But for now, let's look at an example of India's dual linkage in action. In Belize, we referred to Indian people by the nickname Americans used for Chinese people, "Coolie," only without the derogatory connotation.

Here is one of the ways some Indians became Southerners. The British abolished African slavery in 1833. To offset the loss of "their" enslaved Africans, "the demand for Indian indentured laborers increased dramatically . . . They were sent, in large numbers, to plantation colonies . . . in Africa and the Caribbean."[5] One side note to all this: "The British government paid reparations totaling £20 million (equivalent to some £300 billion in 2018) to slave owners when it abolished slavery in 1833."[6] As late as the 1940s, the British and French governments were still repaying loans they made to pay the enslavers.

The final insult is that "the payments went to former slave owners and their descendants, not the enslaved or their legal heirs."[7] That is heartbreaking considering the reactions many in the US have to the word *reparations*, possibly unaware the same political maneuvering happened here. For example, in 1862, Abraham Lincoln signed the "DC Compensated Emancipation Act,"[8] paying enslavers $300 for every enslaved person freed in Washington. And what did those freed Africans receive? They got nothing.

Journalist Pankaj Mishra describes Western attitudes at the time. Westerners believed "the occupation and subjugation of other people's territories were efficacious instruments of civilization."[9] Consider this anomaly that happened during Lord Salisbury's time in British politics. Battles

5. Nationalarchives.gov.uk, "Indian Indentured Laborers," para. 6.

6. Craemer, "There Was a Time Reparations Were Actually Paid Out," para. 11.

7. Craemer, "There Was a Time Reparations Were Actually Paid Out," line 2.

8. Senate.gov, "DC Compensated Emancipation."

9. Mishra, *Bland Fanatics*, 5.

were fought for control of South Africa between two groups of European colonizers. The disagreement was over which of them would rule over the people and seize the gold, diamonds, and anything else of value beneath the ground.

There is something strange about two Western powers fighting each other on African soil. They must have viewed the African people as invisible. One South African author offers proof of this. Alan Paton wrote a seminal novel on South African racism titled *Cry, the Beloved Country.* In it, he suggests that it was the treatment of the Indian population, not the oppression of indigenous Africans, that "brought South Africa into the limelight of the world."[10]

The following example illustrates how Westerners viewed Black people in South Africa. A Boer, a person of Dutch descent, asked Churchill "is it right that a dirty little Kaffir [indigenous African] should walk on the pavement [with whites]—and without a pass too?"[11] Churchill argued that the Kaffirs were better off under British rule than the Boers. But as Churchill biographer Richard Toye records, "The claim that blacks were better off under British rule than the Boers was implausible."[12]

Perhaps a better question would have been, who assigned either of you the task of treating Africans in any particular way? Mishra sheds additional light on the way Westerners viewed Africa. One of his examples is the West's punishment of the Germans following their defeat in the First World War. He writes, "Germany was stripped of its colonies and accused of . . . ill-treating its natives in Africa."[13] Its natives? That is a bizarre perspective, and it explains a lot.

There was another equally bizarre fact. The Boers saw themselves as a legitimate "white South African tribe." They based that belief on the fact that they had occupied the land longer than the British. *Occupied* is the right word too. The two powers claimed ownership of four-fifths of South African land, despite being one-fifth of the population. Who do you think got the most valuable assets? Our friend Nicole tells stories about a colleague who had helped struggling Africans farm. Help was needed because they were forced to scratch out a living on the least farmable soil. This is just one inhumane aspect of the colonial legacy. Here is another.

According to Paton, Europeans extracted tons of gold from African mines. They used the proceeds to build "the biggest hospital south of the

---

10. Paton, *Cry, the Beloved Country,* 15.

11. Toye, *Churchill's Empire,* 68.

12. Toye, *Churchill's Empire,* 69

13. Mishra, *Bland Fanatics,* 54.

Equator."[14] Then they excluded Indigenous Africans from having access. Why would someone even think they had the right to mistreat a group of God's image-bearers in that manner? Is it possible that people who spent centuries believing that kings and queens ruled by divine right simply transferred that right to their race?

HEY, THAT'S MINE!

Now a question for you: "Who owns the rights to what and why?" No, I am not leading you down a path of circular reasoning. I am hoping this will help bring a sense of clarity. If you own your home, how far does your vertical property line extend? Think through this hypothetically. Let us assume you are a nosy neighbor. Would it be okay to fly a drone one thousand feet above your home to see what your neighbors are up to? An incident similar to our hypothetical did occur. During the Cold War, the US decided to spy on Russia. They thought the best way to do it would be to "spy from the sky." But who owns the air and the space above the ground? And secondly, how far should that ownership extend?

In the minds of US officials, Russian air space ended at the limit of their aircraft and missiles' effectiveness. The US had discovered that forty-thousand feet above the ground was about as far as their defense missiles could travel. Then the US developed an aircraft that could cruise at seventy-thousand feet. Presumably, they believed no one had a legitimate claim to the space above the forty-thousand–foot atmospheric property line. It didn't work because the Russians decided against ceding the airspace to the Americans. Instead, they developed technology that could shoot down intruders at the seventy-thousand–foot altitude, and they did. Today they call it the U-2 spy plane incident.

Suppose the question about who owns what and why is asked regarding a nation-state. Do we want to live in a world where an acceptable answer would be whichever one is strong enough to take it? Correspondingly, is it moral for a nation-state to make it legal to own another person if it has the weapons to make it happen? Why not? People have engaged in or condoned that activity in the past, right? I have a close friend who is highly educated, well-traveled, worked in one of the larger churches in Los Angeles, and is white. One day we discussed race concerning what was happening in South Africa after Nelson Mandala became president. He asked me what I thought about Indigenous people, "natives" as he called them, taking away the white ranchers' land.

14. Paton, *Cry, the Beloved Country*, 67.

Truthfully, I did not know what was behind the question. So, I decided to answer the way Jesus did with the Pharisees. I put this question to him in response: "How did the white ranchers come to be owners of that land?" Watching his mind turn as he searched for an answer was fascinating. It was clear he was not comfortable with what he was thinking. He knew the answer was that their forebears saw something they wanted and took it. European settlers first came to the region in the 1600s. They set up shop under the name The Union of South Africa. But, according to Edward Callen, "the framers of the Union failed to agree on a common policy towards the descendants of the conquered African tribes."[15] I'm afraid I have to disagree. They did have a common policy. And as you are about to see, it was based on "what was yours is now ours."

Martin Meredith writes of a time when the European powers were confused about who owned what land in Africa. He was referencing a conference held in Berlin where European powers "carved up ownership" of everything located on the African continent. He mentions a speech by Lord Salisbury when he mockingly states, "We have given away mountains and rivers and lakes to each other, only hindered by the small impediment that we never knew exactly where they were."[16] You cannot get directions when you are far from the land you assigned yourself. My observation is not a joke. It happened!

It is important to understand a few other things about the Berlin conference. Many of the national borders in Africa today result from decisions made at that conference. The Indigenous peoples' concerns mattered little. Thousands of innocent people were imprisoned or executed as a result. The scars that exist because of the insertion of colonial rule will take aeons to heal. Why? Because the intruders hypocritically espoused natural rights. The idea of natural rights stemmed from people like John Locke. He argued that all "people have rights, such as the right to life, liberty, and property."[17] Additionally, he believed natural rights were God-given and nonnegotiable. Despite this, the belief in inferior races led to trampling on those same rights for Africans. One prediction was that under European rule, "Africans will dig ditches and water the deserts . . . [and] probably become extinct."[18] Wow!

According to Meredith, "The Colonial governments were concerned above all to make their territories financially self-supporting."[19] That goal

---

15. Paton, *Cry, the Beloved Country,* 20.

16. Meredith, *Fate of Africa,* 2.

17. Tuckness, "Locke's Political Philosophy," line 4.

18. Lindqvist, *Exterminate All the Brutes,* 131.

19. Meredith, *Fate of Africa,* 3.

was not set to make life better for African people, it was to enrich themselves. The European powers wanted to maximize profit by having Africans pay taxes to them for their own exploitation. So, the colonizers sold some Indigenous leaders on the idea that Africans would provide the raw materials and the labor. And Europeans would collect taxes and reap the profit. Would you trust Western political speak after that? Because of such activities, the racism that contributed to the colonial legacy still acts as a barrier to African global progress.

PEOPLE, PLACES, OR THINGS?

The practice of Europeans claiming ownership of land in Africa led to "10,000 African polities . . . amalgamated into forty European colonies and protectorates."[20] One of the things the African people needed was protection from an invasion by a different colonial power. At least that was how the "benefits" were sold to them. Ethiopia was one of the two African nations not to be conquered by Western powers. The British and the Italians attempted to colonize the country but were unsuccessful. Determined to return to the glory days of the Roman Empire, Italy eventually became its colonial ruler. But it took a brutal invasion that included the use of chemical warfare to do it. Later, Emperor Halie Selassie was able to help take back the country. This achievement was elevated to mythic levels by reggae superstar Bob Marley, and for good reason. What follows explains how that relates to our conversation.

In a speech at the League of Nations, a precursor to our UN, Selassie complained about Italy's aggression toward a people. Notice that he does not refer to Ethiopians as products of an organized nation-state but as a people. He said, "Unequal struggle between a Government commanding more than forty-two million inhabitants, having at its disposal . . . quantities of the most death-dealing weapons [mustard gas], and, on the other hand, a small people of twelve million inhabitants, without arms, without resources having on its side only the justice of its own cause."[21] The point is, in the Southern Hemisphere it is more meaningful to belong to a people than be a citizen of a nation-state. The bond between a people is one of egalitarianism more than allegiance to a flag or national identity. Let us see what "a people" do. And how they dance.

The people of Ethiopia perform a dance called Eskita. That is an African dance known for its shoulder movements "created by observing and

20. Meredith, *Fate of Africa*, 2.
21. Blaisdell, *Great Speeches*, 51.

then imitating the movements made by a snake."[22] One article describes it as similar to the Tigrinya people's dance. Again, that is a dance a *people* enjoy, instead of something done by a specific *nationality*. Remember the concept of kinfolk mentioned in the previous chapter? In the West, it is not unusual to relate to people by geographical origin, not kinship. We think it is perfectly acceptable to say that basketball superstar LeBron James is a "product of Akron, Ohio." We accept this because he was born in that section of America. And we call Michael Jordan a "North Carolina product" because he attended a university in that state. Geography, rather than ancestral lineage, determines personhood in this concept.

Geography, or the land, is central to the African understanding of personhood too, but who you are is not dependent on which political entity controls the land where you are situated. For people in the Southern Hemisphere, identity is about the relationship one has with the people that inhabit the land. In this understanding, land exists to support life instead of being something to fight wars over. I doubt there would be one sportscaster interviewing Jordan or LeBron who would ask, "Who are your people?" in hopes of getting to know them better. However, "Who are your people?" is often the first question an African or Native American will ask a stranger.

A MAN WITH NO NAME

My wife's name is Julaine [Ju-lane]. She and I lived in Belize City, Central America for almost nine years. When we first arrived, it would amuse us to hear people struggle with the pronunciation of Calhoun, our surname. People would say "Cowhun," "Call-on," and a wide array of other strange sounding versions, at least to us. Here is where it gets interesting. Some say the name Belize is "derived from the Spanish pronunciation of the last name of Peter Wallace, a Scottish buccaneer who may have begun a settlement at the mouth of the Belize River about 1638."[23]

Growing up, I assumed my last name was of Irish origin. I joked about being a Black Irishman, unaware that the term was often used as an insult. Today, people invest a lot of time and energy tracing their genealogies and they love to share the findings. My white friends are proud of their European roots, as they should be. However, talking about that stuff hurts because I know my heritage is untraceable. In some ways, I am a person with no name. Sure, there is one that people call me. But it has little meaning

---

22. Danceask.net, "Eskita Dance of Ethiopia," para. 2.

23. Bolland, "Belize," para. 3.

beyond getting my attention. That is because I have no clue when and how it entered my lineage.

Let me ask you a question. Does it rub you the wrong way to learn that a Black person adopts an African or Muslim surname? If it does, why? My wife's family Americanized their Eastern European surnames voluntarily. They were happy to do it. They did it as a sign of belonging. No one viewed them as "rebellious." Yet when Black people shed a name given to them involuntarily, some believe it to be disrespecting America. That is a double standard. Besides, what some view as disrespect might only be the appreciation of something else, such as their historical identity and African self-understanding. Today my name does not define me. However, it was exciting for me to learn that it was originally spelled Colquhoun. The fact it may be of Scottish origin makes it even more interesting. Nevertheless, it is still a name given to me by a European.

That does, however, bring to light one of the challenges of being a person of African descent. I have cultural roots in Africa, Europe, and America. The upside is that I am able to view life in a unique way. Unfortunately, there is a downside. The way race relations are, finding my place in the world can be complicated. In short, I am not a Black Christian and I am not a white Christian. If anything, I am a transracial Christian. Consequently, I am equally comfortable around white and Black Christians, liberal or conservative. That has left many wondering "which side" I am on politically.

But should Christianity have "sides"? In truth, I have much in common with people on all sides. Should God be divided by race? Not really. I am a racial minority in the West, yet I have multiple loyalties. The point is, I am more than one thing. You are more than one thing. And as Oscar Wilde famously said, "Most people are other people. Their thoughts are someone else's opinions, their lives a mimicry."[24] We are composites, so limiting yourself to one perception of anyone is futile and serves no purpose.

OUR SCOTTISH ROOTS–IONA

All of that raises one important question. Should I assume "my people" will have the same skin color as my own? If yes, perhaps this story will cause you to rethink that. Several years ago, we attended a memorial service. Music from the Celtic band Iona was played at the church. The song "Beyond These Shores" moved us deeply, and we purchased more of their music. During a Bridging Austin service, I incorporated an Iona track into the liturgy. A member of our community named Jim asked who made the music. When

24. Goodreads.com, "Oscar Wilde—De Profundis."

I said Iona, he mentioned that John Philip Newell was scheduled to give a presentation in Austin but canceled. I asked who he was, and he answered that he is from Iona.

What came next was life-changing. I thought, okay, John must be a band member. Not remembering the surname, I Googled "Iona musician John." My search produced the name John Bell, a Scottish hymn-writer. Not to be deterred, I checked online to learn more about him. I still didn't find the band, but I found the Iona Community in Scotland. Coincidently, we were looking for a spiritual community whose practices reflected a more inclusive Christian outlook. The Iona Community emphasizes these values.

In the midst of the COVID pandemic, the community was just starting to meet on Zoom. We attended their first meeting and ended up in a chat room with the community's new leader, named Ruth. We both felt a strong connection with her. As a result of that chance meeting, The Iona Community has become a home to us. Its people have become our people. Taking up membership with Iona illustrates that one's "people" do not need to be the result of geography, tribal affiliation, cultural ties, or even blood relations.

CHAPTER 3, PART TWO

Back to Africa

ONE THING THAT NEEDS to be said here is that "dance tells many stories, including those of power and resistance."[1] Much of what we think we know about Africa comes from "Western authors who wrote about that continent without really understanding the cultures in detail."[2] These histories are often incomplete or inaccurate versions of the African story. For example, I only learned about British detention camps in colonial Kenya after I read a book by Caroline Elkin. That tragedy was not common knowledge here in the US. In her book *Imperial Reckonings,* Elkins writes, "I discovered the British had actually detained 1.5 million [Kikuyu] people."[3] "Detained" is more palatable than placed in a prison camp, isn't it?

Indeed, this is hard to accept, considering how fresh the memories of the Nazi concentration camps were in the minds of Western leaders at the time. Why the lack of moral outrage? Because human beings frequently permit themselves to do the things they condemn in others. I cried when I read that Kenyans were forced to wear identification tags around their necks, similar to the tags we place around our dogs' necks. And that happened on the land of their ancestors' birth. Sadly, this proves that, in the words of Paul Valery, "nothing can ever happen again without the whole world's taking a hand."[4] Remember, the "world" in this context is Western

1. Dils and Albright, *Moving History/Dancing Cultures,* 94.
2. Mawusi, *African Theology,* xi.
3. Elkins, *Imperial Reckoning,* xiv.
4. Valery, "Regards sur le monde actuel," para. 8, line 9.

society. We denounced the imprisonment of Jewish people only to allow it to happen to Africans.

Elkins notes "the intense bitterness that was engendered by British colonial rule in Kikuyuland, a bitterness that still seethes today."[5] Edith Turner opens her book about experiencing rituals in Africa with, "We cannot live other people's lives, and it is a piece of bad faith to try . . . We gain [our sense of other people's lives] through their expressions"[6] True, we cannot live other people's lives, but we can have empathy for their suffering and we should. Unfortunately, many of us have a high tolerance for suffering as long as it happens to others. Close your eyes and imagine a foreign power overrunning your country. Now imagine they treated your parents and siblings in a similar fashion. I am confident the emotion that surfaced would not be pity but anger.

The writer Samuel Johnson who once compiled a complete English dictionary, said, "Language is the dress of thought; every time you talk your mind is on parade."[7] African people, on the other hand, often express themselves through music and dance. According to the authors of the book *Way of the Elders*, "Music and dance are the universal languages of the Spirit, communicating its poetry through celebration, ritual, initiation, and healing."[8] As an African theologian suggests, "We cannot explain the culture of people in a few passages, nor can its beauty be well-appreciated even in a volume of books."[9]

That being true, we should look to the people themselves for insight from their perspective. Here is one potential benefit. It would be valuable to understand that when Africans "sing, dance and drum we become in tune with the harmonies of the universe."[10] The spiritual component of African culture should never be overlooked. Materialism is a high priority for people in the West. In the South, material things are but a part of the spiritual world. The material vs. spiritual distinction is not a better or worse proposition. I certainly would not develop a sense of racial superiority because of it. There is no reason why anyone should.

5. Elkins, *Imperial Reckoning*, xiv.

6. Turner, *Experiencing Ritual*, 1.

7. Azquotes.com, "Samuel Johnson."

8. Doumbia and Doumbia, *Way of the Elders*, 95.

9. Mawusi, *African Theology*, 21.

10. Doumbia and Doumbia, *Way of the Elders*, 95.

DANCE RHYTHMS

Music and dance involve rhythm, and life happens in a series of broken rhythms. What I am saying is similar to the biblical "there is a time for everything and a season for every activity under heaven." Therefore, it might be worthwhile to consider some of the meanings behind the rhythms. The rhythms Africans use can have multiple meanings attached. That is because Africans dance as a means of social bonding, rites of passage, preparation for battle, and as part of a religious experience. As the authors referenced in the previous paragraph inform us, "We tell stories through our music and dance."[11] Shortly, I will take you through some of those rhythms and their meanings.

There is one long-standing myth about Africans and people of African descent. That myth says darker-skinned people come equipped with "a natural, biologically innate, unchanging, common response to rhythm."[12] I am sure you have heard a version of that myth. But where did that myth originate? How has it become so firmly planted in the white mind? Folklore and rumor are possibilities, or we can look to the sciences. I am referring to the "ologies," such as biology, anthropology, and ethnology. People use them to explain why difference exists in the human family. Rather than scientifically dissecting a person's heritage, it may be wiser to appreciate how precious "the other" is in the eyes of God. Unfortunately, a natural tension exists between people whose values are rooted in Western science-based culture and the way the rest of the world processes life.

That dichotomy has led to many errant theories advanced by Western "ologists" about what the people are like who occupy the Southern Hemisphere. But the rhythm of life is the focus of this section, so let us get back to that. Regarding African rhythm patterns, Doumbia and Doumbia write, "We have hundreds of rhythms that musicians throughout West Africa must know, and each rhythm tell its own story."[13] Now let us breeze through a small sample of those rhythms. Blues musician Julio Finn writes that "black culture attains its most complete expression in dance."[14] My experience as a funk musician has led me to see it the same way.

First up, there are dances centered around a drum called the djembe. These dances have "a purpose, a time, and a place . . . Some honor groups

---

11. Doumbia and Doumbia, *Way of the Elders*, 96.

12. Baptist, *Half Has Never Been Told*, 16.

13. Doumbia and Doumbia, *Way of the Elders*, 101.

14. Finn, *Bluesman*, 91.

of people."[15] Honoring people as a group aligns with the African concept of personhood. In the West, it is all about the "I." But in the South, it is all about the "we." Peter J. Paris writes, "African understandings of person are always expressed in social terms."[16] The social unit that is revered in every part of Africa is the family. Many Africans will "warn their children to never do anything immoral that would bring a curse or disgrace to the family."[17] That African tradition did not die in the diaspora. My parents drummed a version of that into me as early as I can remember. My family believed ethics have an individual and a collective component. I have held onto that bit of wisdom to this day.

Next in order is the kassa. This one "is a traditional harvest dance and rhythm of the Malinke people. We play this rhythm for those working in the field."[18] One of the materials used to create racial borders is the use of the backward "primitive savage" myth. Imagine how the colonizers probably made fun of Africans banging on drums and dancing as they dug holes to plant crops. Well, dance has a way of flattening the racial superiority curve.

The English also do a dance that is amazingly similar to the Malinke planting dance. It is called the Morris dance or the bean-setting dance. One website describes it for what it is, "a planting dance."[19] Then it tells how the dance is done: "The dancers drill holes using their short sticks as 'dibbers' and then knock the dirt off on the next dancer's stick—or perhaps they pass the 'magic' of the harvest from one to another."[20] Think about all the time and energy invested in trying to prove human beings are essentially different based on a veneer called skin, only to arrive at something like this that shows the opposite is true.

DANCE WITH ARMS WIDE OPEN

Occasionally you run across people who, driven by loving hearts, are willing to dance intimately with the stranger. Meet Iain and Isabel Whyte. In the 1970s, they were two young people who had committed their lives to pursuing justice and peace for marginalized people. If dance involves moving one's body, their lives can be a shining example. Isabel and Iain were willing to move their bodies nearly 4,500 miles to Ghana, West Africa, to

15. Doumbia and Doumbia, *Way of the Elders*, 101.

16. Paris, *Spirituality*, 101.

17. Mawusi, *African Theology*, 125.

18. Doumbia and Doumbia, *Way of the Elders*, 103.

19. Morrisdances.com, "Bean Setting," line 1.

20. Morrisdances.com, "Bean Setting," line 1.

effect social change for people they had not met. What holds many of us back from any meaningful involvement in the lives of others is fear. That is a programmed reaction to the sight of dark skin for many. But is fear always warranted?

According to Mark Mathabane, the darker-skinned South African attitude towards white people in his area is, "If you're introduced to the community and show them respect instead of pitying them, they will protect you even with their own lives."[21] If you are a white person, would you imagine that is how you would be treated in an African setting? What about that "bad neighborhood" populated by darker-skinned people in an average American city? Remember my friend Carl Faraone from the first chapter? He could walk down any street in "the hood" without fear any time he wanted, and he did. What if the idea that any white person found in a Black neighborhood would immediately be attacked is a myth? One that was developed over time by people who had never even been in one? That is possible, right? Now back to our story.

When the Whytes landed in Ghana, Isabel was a young white mother surrounded by Black people. Soon after their arrival Isabel became ill. They had no car and no way of traveling into town for her to get medical treatment. What did she do? She went to the nearest thoroughfare and hitchhiked in! That required her to trust the people group in a general sense. She also needed to trust the stranger that would offer her a ride. To portray Isabel accurately, let me utilize a rarely used noun, "truster." The word is defined as you would expect, a "firm belief in the integrity, ability, or character of a person."[22] Isabel was a truster, and she had no problem doing that because it came naturally to her. Iain told us the following story that demonstrates what truster means.

Isabel would frequently leave her son in the care of her African neighbors. Her view differed from many Europeans who arrived in Africa and perceived their hospitality as de facto hired help. She viewed them as neighbors in the African sense. The African way is where children are a responsibility of the community. This is very important. There are darker-skinned people in every city, right? That means you do not have to go to Ghana to form relationships with Black people. Are you as willing to be a "truster" of them as Isabel was to her African friends? Be honest.

Iain and Isabel lived in an eight-unit apartment building, and they were the only white people there. They had not been in Africa long when Isabel became pregnant. The Ghanaians have a custom that when a child

21. Mathabane, *Lessons of Ubuntu*, 247.
22. Thefreedictionary.com, "Truster."

is born into a family, the community acknowledges there is an additional mouth to feed. And out of their meager resources, the Ghanaians took up a collection and presented it to Isabel. They did this knowing that she was better off than them in a financial sense. But for the people of Ghana, "helping a needy member of the community" is the mark of a good citizen. These people welcomed this "Whyte couple" from Scotland into their community as full members.

Sadly, we recently lost Isabel, and her eulogy contained the following words: "People mattered to her more than anything." The Ghanaian people sensed that about her. That is why they loved her. That is also why Julaine and I loved her so much. The main takeaway from this chapter and Isabel's story is this: Making the other person matter to you is the most effective way to achieve lasting results when you want to resolve conflict. If you were to see the world like Isabel, you would never need to argue about whose lives matter the most.

CHAPTER 4, PART ONE

The East

"I am the East. I have philosophies, I have religions."[1]

—AMEEN RIHANI

CHINA

CHINA AND INDIA ARE nations that are home to a variety of cultures and religions. As ancient civilizations, both China and India share many similarities and an equal amount of differences. I apologize that space does not allow us to touch on even a tiny portion of them. With that in mind, let us begin with China. Musicologist Curt Sachs writes, "For the Chinese, cosmic harmony originates in the dance; planets and gods swing through the universe in the dance."[2] A renowned kung fu master once referred to the Chinese martial art tai chi as "dancing." He based that opinion on its highly choreographed body movements and synchronized footwork. If you have watched tai chi, you know it uses extremely slow and graceful movements. In fact, the action is so slow that it can appear to those watching to be inaction.

Today mixed martial arts are popular. Their frenetic pace makes it understandable that tai chi in contrast could be seen as a fitness program for seniors. Concurrently, others see it as an activity done in a park that facilitates meditation. But if tai chi is an exercise program that resembles dance,

---

1. Azquotes.com, "Ameen Rihani."
2. Sachs, *World History,* 6.

its movements can prepare the dancer for war. That is true even when done in a group. That is because tai chi is a deadly martial art in addition to its patterned routines. I have practiced more than one martial art, and I can assure you that slow, well-focused movements can achieve desired outcomes. The same process could bring about success in racial reconciliation, faith, and international diplomacy, if applied.

China's political leaders have used similar tactics regarding their role as a rising global power. I say this because, leading up to the Korean War, China did not see itself as a major player on the world stage. They believed the USA and Russia were major players, but not themselves. A former director of the People's Liberation Army said this about the Korean conflict: "The enemy came to our doorstep, and they forced us to enter the war."[3] Most students who sign up for a kung fu class will hear a variation of this one idea. Martial artists don't start fights; they end them.

China's recent past is one of unity followed by war. Then they experienced a time of peace followed by political turmoil. And "this left China significantly weakened and subject to invasion and Western humiliation."[4] These factors caused Chinese diplomacy to take a different path called "wolf warrior." Its strategic bottom line is this: "We never pick a fight or bully others, but . . . we will push back against any deliberate insult, resolutely defend our national honor and dignity."[5] That is similar to practicing tai chi and a posture one assumes when anticipating conflict. In simple terms, they are ready to prevent being bullied. Before this shift, many believed China held a similar political theory to Russia. That would be a communist ideology that produces expansionist tendencies.

However, if true, China came to an entirely different conclusion at some point. And that is, "The best defense is, well, a good defense." That posture starkly contrasted with Russia's, which we will discuss later. This defense-oriented emphasis led to the belief that an insular society was the best route for protecting the Chinese people. Even though China is gradually opening its society, it remains pretty closed. That may be because the colonial era had established "good government" as being the type that had the approval of Western powers.

As far as the Western powers were concerned, any attempt by the Chinese or other subjugated populations to achieve self-determination was aggressive. And aggression was a euphemism for any demand Asian people made for the dignity of self-rule. But Western "permission" isn't all I am

---

3. Conrad, "70 years on, how China sees the Korean War," para. 6.

4. Hejazi, "Lessons in Chinese History," para. 5.

5. Westcott and Jiang, "Here's what wolf warrior diplomacy means," para. 3.

highlighting here. The importance of respecting basic sovereignty is what I'm stressing. That was not always a given for people in the East. As a result, using Western sources to gauge Chinese goals or intentions can be misleading. Should you desire to learn more, I suggest you start with the Paris Peace Conference that followed the First World War. There the values and interests of Western powers were on full display.

Shortly we will examine dance in China with an eye toward better understanding the political minds of over a billion Chinese citizens. When I use the phrase "political minds," I do not mean those of the nation's political leaders but the minds of the people affected by them. Here is one example. Bryan Van Norden writes, "Traditional Chinese culture was never democratic but always emphasized the well-being and happiness of the people as the ultimate arbiter of political legitimacy."[6] Let us assume Van Norden's use of the word *traditional* to be synonymous with historical. Then to better understand the people's attitudes today, it would be wise to study the dances and religions of China's past.

"A king can be judged by the condition of dancing during his reign."[7]

—CHINESE PROVERB

China is an ancient society with a rich political history. It is also home to an equally glamorous cultural past. During much of that history China was an agrarian society. The country's economic well-being depended on the success of its farming. That caused rainfall to become a top concern of religious and political leaders. Van Norden notes that a person named Shen Nong introduced agriculture to the people. And with that, the people learned "to plant crops, domesticate animals,"[8] and form communities. In Psalm 131, a question is raised that is as important now as it was then: "Where does my help come from?"[9] Then as now, people turned to religion and politics to answer that question. Let us look at the resources that the Chinese people turned to in times of need.

A shaman was a religious leader in China during that period. The shaman was the "person regarded as having access to, and influence in, the world of good and evil spirits, especially among some peoples of northern Asia."[10] Sachs writes, "In advanced Chinese culture—in the first millennium

6. Van Norden, *Classical Chinese Philosophy*, 4.

7. Terry, *Invitation to Dance*, 164.

8. Van Norden, *Classical Chinese Philosophy*,, 3.

9. Ps 121:1, NIV.

10. Lexico.com, "Shaman."

before Christ—the shaman must make rain in ecstatic dance."[11] Then he describes what that dance may have looked like. He writes, "The rainmaker heaps a pile of stones or sand, places a magic stone on top, and for hours at a time dances around the stone chanting magic words."[12] Let's put that in a different context than farming. According to one book on Asian studies, "land and water have also been important markers of spiritual and political significance."[13]

So, people in China looked to religion to meet their needs, and when they needed water, they danced for it. There came a time when they turned to politics to gain control over the very thing they had danced before the gods to provide. But that change of direction was still about water. Van Norden writes of a time when flooding caused problems for the people. An emperor named Shun created a "centralized government with the resources to organize massive irrigation, flood control and canal building projects."[14] That they looked to a shaman and then the emperor demonstrates that religion and politics have been linked for much longer than we realize.

Shun's decisions achieved the desired goal and temporarily saved the day. In some cases, that is what politicians do—provide short-term solutions. As we have been discussing, many people believe that religion and politics can provide all the security that they need in life. That has been true of humankind from the very beginning. But then as now, people can rely too heavily on politics. They can also ask more of religion than it claims. That makes it difficult to differentiate between the proper role of one or both. That is especially true during times of stress. That being the case, let us take our mind off of that and look at dance. We are about to see that even when the people's primary concern was food and survival, they still managed to dance.

"If you are going to walk on thin ice, you might as well dance."[15]

—CHINESE PROVERB

In the US, breaking the ice means to "break down a social stiffness in order for things to be more comfortable."[16] Chinese people used dance as a means of overcoming fear and inhibitions. To express an idea similar to the proverb

11. Sachs, *World History,* 64.

12. Sachs, *World History,* 64.

13. Spencer et al., *Checkpoint, Temple, Church and Mosque,* 47.

14. Van Norden, *Classical Chinese Philosophy,* 4.

15. Inspirationalstories.com, "Chinese Proverbs On Dancing."

16 Knowyourphrase.com, "Break the Ice."

above, we might say "go for it," or "throw caution to the wind." One of the ways they did that was similar to what I witnessed during my sex, drugs, and rock and roll years. For example, Sachs writes of a "spring dance" that the people of the eastern region of China did. That was where "unmarried boys and girls dance in couples, grasping each other by the hips; at the conclusion of the dance the girls are lifted onto the backs of boys and carried away."[17]

That type of dancing also sounds like the "rolling" slow dance that African Americans engaged in at the house parties I mentioned earlier. Sachs then says, "One cannot always divide erotic dances into a reserved first movement and the execution of the act [actual intercourse] in a second movement."[18] To be clear, my reason for including this is not sex but intimacy. The fear of being intimate with people different from you is the source of a whole lot of misery.

Let us think about some possible applications for this type of "intimacy" in today's church. The fact that people are willing to engage in sex with a stranger suggests two things. One, we are wired towards intimacy if motivated. Two, it is possible to let go of inhibitions in return for the promise of pleasure. When we fail to love the stranger, it is more about our lack of motivation than whether they are Black, a Republican, or an immigrant. For a while, affinity groups were the rage in churches. The thinking was that relationships are more likely to blossom when people share something in common. It didn't work. Small groups based on this idea were no more successful than other types.

The problem was fear of intimacy and not the program itself. The motivation to love for Christians should also be pleasure, just not the personal kind. The kind of pleasure I am speaking of is found in pleasing God. Jesus said where your treasure is, there is your heart. We tend to treasure the things that please us. But if you treasure God, you will find pleasure there. Psalm 16:11 says it this way: "You make known to me the path of life; you will fill me with joy in your presence, with eternal pleasures at your right hand." At the close of the epilogue, I will say more about the heart and why attention to it is critical.

KOREA

Like China's, Korean dance has a long history that makes it challenging to identify which styles of dance best represent Korean culture. According to Dils and Albright, "The variety of dances classified by Koreans as traditional

17. Sachs, *World History*, 66.
18. Sachs, *World History*, 66.

dances differ in both the contexts and manners in which they were originally performed."[19] Despite them being East Asian culturally, Westerners
will describe the Indigenous people as being South or North Korean. I live
in Texas, so I can only wonder if these distinctions reflect actual differences.
It is not easy to know how people see themselves. That should give us pause.
Why? Because, in most cases, people desire to be recognized for who they
are, not for what others say.

Just think, many nations were formed by politicians drawing lines on
a map and assigning nationality to anyone living within them. As with unnatural racial categories, these assignments happen without thought given
to tribal affiliation, cultural identity, or local history. Many argue that being
Korean-born is not the same as being culturally Korean. A scientific study
claims, "Koreans are more closely related to the Japanese and quite distant
from the Chinese."[20] Yet, when it comes to dance, Judy Van Zile suggests
that because of "political interactions between China and Korea,"[21] many of
the Korean court dances borrowed heavily from China. This is why there
are large numbers of dances to choose from in "historical Korea." Out of the
many, I settle on two, the Nun Dance and the Dance of the Court.

THE DANCES

The Nun Dance, called the *Sungmu,* is a very popular dance. According to
professor Lee Kyong-Hee, a leading *Sungmu* performer says it "embodies
not only the basic structure of Korean traditional folk dance but also the
stream of our national history."[22] Lee explains that *Sungmu* "stands for our
traditional philosophy of heaven and earth and their harmony."[23] This leads
to a topic we seldom discuss in American churches—the seamless relationship between heaven and earth. When Rabbi Jesus prayed, "Your will be
done on earth as it is in heaven,"[24] was that an unrealistic proposition? Or
are we called to participate in the specific mission to "create peace, then
build a bridge, and, finally marry heaven and earth."[25]

19. Dils and Albright, *Moving History/Dancing Cultures,* 178.

20 Saha and Tay, "Origin of the Koreans," line 8.

21. Dils and Albright, *Moving History/Dancing Cultures,* 179.

22. Dils and Albright, *Moving History/Dancing Cultures,* 174.

23. Dils and Albright, *Moving History/Dancing Cultures,* 175.

24. Matt 6:10, NIV.

25. Chabadgreenwich.org, "Heaven and Earth," line 18.

Korean monks received "training in the musical chanting of scriptures and dance performance"[26] in pursuit of the Buddhist understanding of peace. Perhaps it would be helpful for Christians to follow suit. Imagine what it would be like to dance and sing the Scriptures to promote political peace. Is it possible to elevate spiritual matters above political division in the church for the sake of social harmony? Sometimes I wonder whether it would be cool to walk into a local church next Sunday and find half the congregation dancing and singing. I certainly think so, and it might, in the process, bring heaven a little closer to earth in the minds of some. We will discuss that possibility shortly.

The second dance is performed around a large drum that people beat to the accompaniment of an orchestra. Sometimes it involves twelve other performers who dance around the four winds that blow north, south, east, and west. Other Korean dances are based on multiples of four as well. The point is, Korea's traditional dances are very well structured and organized. There are no borders to traditional dances either. Since this was a dance of "the court," meaning the seat of power, styles would change with the direction of the political winds.

UNINVITED DANCERS

Border crossings are not always cause to celebrate. Japan's decision to invade Korea is one of those instances. When the Japanese colonized Korea in 1910, "there were periods when Japan made every effort to obliterate traditional Korean culture."[27] In response to being subjugated by their neighbors, the Korean people developed mask dances "to poke fun at things"[28] in protest. Dances that were perceived as good-natured fun were actually ritualized expressions of hostility. Why were the Japanese people so oppressive? Allow me to answer by analogy.

At one time I smoked and drank heavily. Both habits were difficult to break. There is a saying that an "ex-anything" is the most intolerant person you will ever encounter. I found that true of ex-druggies and ex-alcoholics. Before the period under discussion, the Japanese had been an isolated people for hundreds of years. The everyday citizens, known as peasants, were oppressed. Over time, this feudal island country became an empire. Once the powerless attain power, they can become oppressive. This was true of the

26. Dils and Albright, *Moving History/Dancing Cultures,* 176.

27. Dils and Albright, *Moving History/Dancing Cultures,* 184.

28. Dils and Albright, *Moving History/Dancing Cultures,* 180.

Japanese. As "the ex-oppressed," they became the least tolerant people in the region, becoming oppressors themselves.

Benedict Anderson notes, "If it is permissible for the working-class [in places like Russia] to unite to overthrow unjust authority by bloodshed, then unconditional approval should be given to Japan to . . . make war for the rectification of unjust international frontiers."[29] And they did. The Japanese colonized "Taiwan, Korea, Karafuto and Kuril Islands, Islands of the Pacific Ocean, Manchuria, and China."[30] And they behaved in much the same way as the colonizers in the previous chapters, except more intensely. Anderson writes, "Japanified Koreans, Taiwanese or Burmese had their passage to the metropole [the parent state of a colony] absolutely barred."[31] There is a thread that connects people in the East and the South during times of suffering. When people are oppressed, they bang on drums and dance.

29. Anderson, *Imagined Communities*, 98.

30. Jluggage.com, "Countries Japan Colonized," para. 1.

31. Anderson, *Imagined Communities*, 99.

CHAPTER 4, PART TWO

India

COLONIZATION IS JUST A horrible idea at a humanitarian level. It seems to result in politicians proposing laws to improve the colonizers' lives, causing others to suffer due to those same laws. A prime example of this is on display in the British television series *The Crown*. In one scene, a foe of the English royal family quipped, "That bloody Lord Mountbatten gave away *our* India." That was about the decision by the British to "let" the Indigenous people of the region have political freedom. This was after many years of Western colonial rule. The purpose of colonial rule was not to improve the quality of life for Indians. On the contrary, the way it was done caused a significant problem for the majority of them.

Once again some border lines were drawn by a politician who had never set foot in that country. Then "a bloody partition was set with the decision to sever Bengal in the east and Punjab in the west in half-giving Jinnah what he called a 'moth-eaten Pakistan.'"[1] The result was "the slaughter of more than a million people; some 15 million were displaced. Untold numbers were maimed, mutilated, dismembered, and disfigured. Countless lives were scarred."[2] When reading about colonialism's aftereffects such as these, I ask myself, "What brought this about?" Have you thought about why people felt justified in the behavior that led to so much suffering?

1. Najam, "Conversation," para. 23.
2. Najam, "Conversation," para. 2.

DANCING IN KERALA

There is a fascinating book, *Nine Lives,* written by an award-winning Scottish writer named William Dalrymple. The book recounts his adventures traveling in the India that remained after it was "given back" to the Indigenous people. I lifted the following words from a blurb on the author's page on Amazon.com. It summarizes the parts of his book that I will be commenting on: "A Buddhist monk takes up arms to resist the Chinese invasion of Tibet . . . A Jain nun tests her powers of detachment as she watches her closest friend ritually starve herself to death . . . [And] a prison warder from Kerala is worshipped as an incarnate deity for three months of every year."

Dalrymple gives us insight into the mind of a Theyyam dancer from Kerala named Hari Das. Theyyam is fascinating. That is because it combines music and dance to make a value judgment. It can contrast the spiritual with the political. This description of Theyyam is from the region's tourism web page: "Theyyam is a famous ritual art form that . . . brings to life the great stories of our State."[3] Das "sees Theyyam as a tool and a weapon to fight back against an unjust social system as much as a religious revelation."[4]

It moved me to hear our dancer speak these words: "If you pray to God with a sincere heart and focus . . . so that you can see nothing but what you are aiming at . . . from that moment on it is not the dancer who dances, but the god."[5] The ability to focus on that level is desirable when practicing tai chi and dancing Theyyam. I wish more Western Christians understood that to focus entirely on God is not weirdness but the proper response to the God who exists. I will go deeper into that later, but for now, let us turn to the political aspect.

During another conversation with Das, Dalrymple asked our spiritual dancer this question, "Is this a full-time job, becoming a god?"[6] Hari answered no, then explained that he worked as a day laborer and correctional officer when he was not dancing for the gods. Das described how dangerous and violent it was for the prisoners and guards inside the jail. He said the reason was "all you have to do all day is wander around with a lathi [cane] and avoid getting knifed."[7] Politics was at the core of the conflict between the inmates. Politics run deep, and the Keralans will cut off the noses and ears of their political opponents in a heartbeat.

3. Keralatourism.org, "Theyyam Ritual Artform," line 1.

4. Dalrymple, *Nine Lives,* 37.

5. Dalrymple, *Nine Lives,* 44.

6. Dalrymple, *Nine Lives,* 32.

7. Dalrymple, *Nine Lives,* 45.

Before you become too judgmental about them, remember how divided our politics have become. Thankfully, I haven't seen anyone cut off an ear. But I have seen people cut off relationships with political opponents. Some of my clergy peers have also said they hope people who refuse vaccination get infected and die, presumably thinking there would be one less person capable of infecting others. One wished a kid firing an assault rifle in Wisconsin would have shot more protestors. Yet another said he wished someone would kill a foreign head of state because he did not like that country's policies. Pastors made those comments. Extreme? Yes! Is that typical of these times? Unfortunately, yes again. But Jesus calls us to love our enemies, not wish them harm.

RUSSIA

As we end our dance through the East, I want to share what I thought I knew about Russia. A pair of respected scholars wrote, "Russians have generally viewed the United States as a strategic guide and model . . . Moscow's posture has been that of reaction to US capabilities."[8] That sums up what I grew up believing. Russians were after us, and we needed to stay one step ahead of them or we'd be in big trouble. Fear of the "Russian bear" has remained a constant. All an American has to do to strike fear in another American is mention a Russian. That they are a rival to us is all I knew about Russia. I was unaware of its contribution to the art of dance. Now instead of discussing Russian ballistic missiles or bombs, we can discuss ballet. To do that, we will look at the work of a Russian choreographer named Leonid Yakobson. Dance provided this artistic genius a way to express his feelings about Russia's autocratic government.

If I were to ask, "What do ballet and bombs have in common?," how would you answer? Janet Ross, a dance scholar at Stanford University, wrote the seminal book on the life of Yakobson [Jacobson]. Her title weds our mutually incompatible words "bomb and ballet" this way: *Like a Bomb Going Off: Leonid Yakobson and Ballet as Resistance in Soviet Russia.* I want our focus to be on one of the other words in that title. That word is *resistance.* That is because Yakobson's "ballets challenged the role of the dancing body during some of the most repressive decades of totalitarian rule."[9] Additionally, the ballets of Yakobson criticized the state despite laws against it. Many people described their political impact as a bomb going off, hence the book's title. I, for one, never knew ballet could speak, let alone protest.

8. Solomon and Kosaka, *Soviet Far East Buildup*, 21.

9. Ross, *Like a Bomb Going Off*, 7.

If you have ever witnessed an American square dance, then you know two things. There are people doing the steps on the floor. Then another person tells them how, when, and where to step. The person giving the prompts is known as a "caller." A person who fills the same role in ballet is called a choreographer. Leonid Yakobson was just such a person. Ross writes that he used dance as "the ultimate stealth art form—his ballets can appear complacent and docile on the surface while just below they display an aggressive aesthetic that challenges the status quo."[10] Yakobson believed that dancing bodies reflected the values and mood of a culture. He also saw dance as influencing culture.

Ross writes later in the book that "the twinning of political power and classical ballet has a long and unique alignment in Russia."[11] She further states, "It is only by beginning to understand what ballet signified in Soviet Russia that one can understand why Yakobson's works were so threatening."[12] Dances done by those with less social power seem to be perceived as a threat to those with more. That is true regardless of which type of political system is in operation. The reason is that dance is a viable form of protest. Korean ritual dancers, a Russian choreographer, and enslaved Africans prove that.

KNOW YOUR LIMITS

Ballet and tai chi dancers must develop specific skills to succeed. They need to be aware of what is happening around them. They also need to be sensitive to other dancers' moves. The same is true of nations that qualify as superpowers. I remember the disco dancing craze of the late 1970s. For you who are too young to remember, perhaps you have seen the movie *Saturday Night Fever*. The plot revolves around a couple dedicated to dance. The dancers practice their moves night and day to gain the approval of their peers. When a movie is successful, there are spin-offs and spoofs that follow. That happened here because there was a comedy version of that movie. The male lead was not the cool, handsome, and suave John Travolta. No, the main character in this film was a geek.

In this film the lead actor was nerdy and awkward. His dance skills impressed no one. In fact this guy couldn't dance at all. Once on the dance floor, he would make klutzy moves that got people's attention for the wrong reason. The people watching spent most of their time laughing at him. The more they laughed, the more he exaggerated his dorky dance steps. You see,

10. Ross, *Like a Bomb Going Off*, 3.

11. Ross, *Like a Bomb Going Off*, 25.

12. Ross, *Like a Bomb Going Off*, 25.

he was clueless about the reason behind the laughter. That illustrates what it is like not to be self-aware. When a dancer moves in ways that are outside the norm, it can be amusing. When a nation behaves in the same way as our clueless dancer, it is not so funny.

A CHOREOGRAPHY OF ALTRUISM

As we close, remember that the goal of this book is to hold what is different in contrast. Westerners take it for granted that Russia and China's view of power differs from Europe and America's. Before agreeing with that assessment, Google "list of invasions" and it should lead to a Wikipedia article. There you will find some statistics that will shock you. Provided the article is accurate, Western powers have in fact invaded more nations than Russia or China. I pointed you to the article because I wanted you to be able to read the stats for yourself. However, my point is not about the violence but perception. I am referring to the type of perception that causes a nation-state, or person, to not see "the log in their own eyes."

My writings are theological and sociological and not political. Many of my peers filter their theological or sociological opinions through political lenses. As an example, let us consider the issue of race. In the US, much has been written about the perceived intolerance of Trump supporters. On the other side, people write about the failures of the Democrats through the Obama years. The truth is, racial issues do not stem from either. The challenges we face are due to a failure of the heart. And if you are a Christian, then a failure of the Christian heart. Displacing politics as the "go-to" mechanism for resolving social conflicts would lead to a less adversarial response to them.

To all of us living in the West, especially those in the US and the UK, consider this hypothetical. Let us say China occupied the US and Russia annexed Western Europe. We are all forced to live under completely different political systems. The result is our lives are changed dramatically. Just think, the conflicts between friends and family might decrease without political disagreements. And Christians would see God's plans in a different way, without politics driving the agenda. Finally, what would your priorities be in this scenario?

In this chapter we have discussed two types of choreography, Russian ballet and Chinese tai chi. Altruism is defined as "selfless concern for the well-being of others."[13] The dictionary defines choreography as a "sequence

---

13. Lexico.com, "Altruism."

of steps and movements."[14] I propose we use these two words, and their definitions, as a template for loving others. The principle could be called "the choreography of altruism."

For a picture of what that looks like we can turn to John Harper. He was a Scottish minister traveling to the US on the Titanic when it sank. What steps did he take? He stepped away from the possibility of safety to move toward the certainty of death. How? When the ship hit the iceberg, Harper picked up his young daughter and placed her on a lifeboat. Then he selflessly chose to stay on a sinking ship to bring comfort to those about to die. That is what love does, it puts others first. Love is what defines a Christian. Now I invite you to create your own sequence of steps and movements that result in a selfless concern for the well-being of others.

14. Lexico.com, "Choreography."

SECTION TWO

Race

"I care about the human race, and I strive to understand it."[15]

—JANICE TANTON

15. Picturequotes.com, "Janice Tanton."

CHAPTER 5, PART ONE

Whiteness

THINKING AND SEEING DIFFERENTLY

WHAT I HOPE TO show in this chapter is that for a society to exhibit values that are Christlike, "People must be united; they must dissolve all internal divisions . . . and they must have legal equality."[1] In light of that, let us examine something written about early American society: "In the wake of the Revolutionary War, race and citizenship remained closely tied together . . . The original concept of citizenship as a grouping of equal individuals restricted membership to white males."[2] What we see in that statement is the birth of what many call, sometimes pejoratively, identity politics.

The Oxford dictionary describes identity politics as "a tendency for people of a particular religion, race, social background, etc., to form exclusive political alliances."[3] One example is that there was a law in 1790 that limited naturalized US citizenship to "free white persons." Subsequent to that law, "the racial restriction was not eliminated entirely until 1952."[4] Every nation-state requires a group identity to promote peaceful and cohesive community life. However, that can lead to discrimination. And no matter

1. Hutchinson and Smith, *Nationalism*, 4.
2. Wolfe, "Race and Citizenship," para. 5.
3. Lexico.com, "Identity politics."
4. Immigrationhistory.org, "Nationality Act of 1790," para. 1.

how often some would deny it, discrimination has always been part of our sociopolitical foundation. This is one area where getting history right is very important. Here is why.

Some people become offended at the mere mention of the phrase *identity politics*. The reason is they believe it causes more harm than good. If that is you, I ask you to "give it another think," as my Scottish friends say. That is because the American "settlers" crafted political systems using one specific identity as their foundation. That identity was the white male. Then legislation affirming their privileged position followed. For example, at the time of its charter in 1629, only freemen, meaning white males, had standing and could participate in government in the Massachusetts Bay Colony. The dictionary defines standing as "status or position . . . in a community."[5] We would call that full citizenship today.

In that social arrangement, many people lived with fewer rights than white male property owners, including white women, children, and the white working class. One hundred years after the founding, the fifteenth amendment gave all men the right to vote. Women were given the right fifty years later. However, the "all" did not include Black men. This is the type of internal division that is of concern in this section. For hundreds of years, "Whiteness has been the invisible norm in the West, a transparent, yet ubiquitous frame of reference so pervasive that most Whites consider themselves absolved from race matters."[6] That indicates most white people assume matters of race pertain to non-white people, not themselves. If a race problem exists, it is *their* problem. That is so because whiteness frequently critiques and evaluates others while refusing to do the same to itself.

Similar to a virus, racial superiority can infect an entire society. At this stage, whiteness becomes more than an identity, it takes on the role of a self-validating ideology. More importantly, whiteness then determines who and what is right in most areas of life. Soon disagreements between racial groups about whose political rights should be protected the most surface. For example, let us imagine it is 1860. Should white people's right to own and control other people be preserved? Or should Black people's right to freedom and equality take precedence?

Remember Locke's God-decreed formula of the right to life, liberty, and property? His views on rights could lead to this conclusion. The only way a person can own something is when they are free. But granting freedom second would place property rights last. This exposes the problem with rights-based ethics. When racial ideology controls the distribution of rights,

5. Lexico.com, "Standing."
6. Hill, *Whiteness,* back cover.

everyone pays a price. Ideas such as "just enslavement" can follow. For example, enslaved Africans were born into lives that lacked basic human rights and then passed on that status to the not yet born. That was neither just nor right! We must shift our focus from rights, to doing the right thing concerning race. Hopefully, this will get you thinking about how.

To calibrate means to determine or track the progress of something. Current anti-racism rhetoric must be recalibrated. To this point it has focused on the activity and not the result. This sidesteps the pain and suffering involved. Then race relations are framed in a way that makes them appear better than they are. In America, large numbers of people underestimate the depths of racism. As a result, race issues are not discussed in many circles, allowing indifference to prevail. But things would change if more people would let go of their romanticized version of race relations. Try this exercise. Get a blank sheet of paper and list the ways you believe race relations are better. Now cite the evidence you have for each item. I suspect it was hard to find evidence to match your beliefs.

CULTURAL BEINGS OR RACIAL BEINGS?

We have just made our way through various cultures' dances. Let me take a moment to define *culture*. Culture is the sum total of activities engaged in by a specific group of people. Those activities include choices in food, dress, language, religion, and, yes, dance. But this definition cannot determine what it means to be a racial being in a society. For there to be racial beings, some type of narrative must be in place to prove they exist. That narrative must also be elastic, i.e., plausible enough, to convince people that race is a biological fact.

Once established, people accept that differences between races exist because of evolution, God, or one group winning life's lottery. South African colonizer Cecil Rhodes said, "Remember that you are an Englishman, and consequently won first prize in the lottery of life."[7] At this point, "race is transformed into a real phenomenon which has identifiable effects in the social world."[8] Many believe the winning and losing brackets in life's game of chance, a.k.a. racial hierarchies, should remain in place forever. That perception equates to a losing lottery ticket being acceptable for some folks. Every game has a winner and a loser, and there is no midway in sport or race. What follows exposes one of the underpinnings of that attitude.

7. Brainyquote.com, "Cecil Rhodes."
8. Daynes and Lee, *Desire for Race*, 54.

I remember a scene in a popular American television series where a man asks a relative what he thinks Jesus looks like. The father-in-law responds that he looks like "a regular white guy, just like all the pictures." I include this not to criticize the depictions but to highlight their repercussions. Many people believe these artist renderings reflect the appearance of the historical Jesus. But that reduces God to a racial category. Additionally, connecting "God in the flesh" to whiteness causes white to be seen as the regular skin tone for a human being. One of my Facebook friends posted a picture of a man dressed in a white robe with straw-blond hair playing the tuba. Her comment on the post read, "I didn't know Jesus plays an instrument." Here is the problem. If whiteness is the norm, then non-whiteness will be understood as abnormal or, at minimum, a variant.

One tragic repercussion of this mindset was the eugenics movement. It sought to medically create a white master race by controlling the reproductive rights of darker-skinned people, people living with a disability, and those deemed atypical in some way. Yes, it happened, and it could happen again. A behavioral geneticist recently published a book titled *The Genetic Lottery: What DNA Means for Social Inequality.* People think of race when they hear the word *inequality* in the US, don't they? The title suggests that genetics can somehow help eliminate inequality. Do you believe some people are born superior? Do you think it is possible to "fix" those who are not? If yes, please remember the Nazis in Germany tried that science. It did not end well!

MODELING

Clinical psychologist Peter Miller believes "individuals learn by observing the behaviors of others (models)."[9] Modeling is the process of projecting one's ideals onto others in order to shape them into a predetermined mold. I have applied this theory to create something I call "racial modeling." You can see racial modeling in action the way that the media portrays whiteness juxtaposed with Blackness. They represent whiteness as virtuous, entrepreneurial, hardworking, brave, and capable.

In contrast, Blackness is depicted as artistic, athletic, and frequently criminal (in the case of men). The people promoting these stereotypes claim that they don't value one group over the other. They say they are only showing the American public what we are really like. But as Mike Hill points out in *Whiteness*, in the United States, "the system of racial categories is

9. Miller, *Principles of Addiction,* 293.

bookended by whiteness and blackness."[10] That says white and Black people are not viewed as similar but mutually exclusive opposites.

Quite often crime is not viewed equally but in Black and white. A recent tragedy in Buffalo, New York helps to illustrate this point. A white nineteen-year-old male shot thirteen people, killing ten African Americans. Even though the legal age of accountability was eighteen, a white pastor friend of mine wrote a long exposé painting the shooter as a "kid." In it he informs his readers this teenager's brain is still developing. Is he implying that an underdeveloped brain, even if true, lessens the impact of the "kid's" brutality? In Florida, a white teenager who killed seventeen people escaped the death penalty by way of the same logic.

Now compare my pastor friend's characterization with words used by a prosecutor to describe a Black fourteen-year-old who killed one six-year-old. This kid smothered the girl to death while trying out wrestling moves that he had seen on television. Assistant State Attorney Ken Padowitz said, "This was a brutal, savage beating."[11] To be clear, I am not addressing the severity of each crime. I am drawing your attention to the reaction racially. Why is there no compassion for the Black teen, as with the white perpetrators? Instead, we have a rush to revulsion and the use of the "savage" metaphor. What makes people emote differently depending on the "race" of the victim or the perpetrator? We will look more at savagery in a moment. For now, let us continue with how crime is perceived according to skin color.

SHIM, SHAM, SHIMMY

For starters, the shim-sham and the shimmy are dances. But what follows is not about the dances per se, only the ideas that flow from their names. Now, let us discuss them in order. Shims are devices that make an item fit the way you desire. For example, a shim makes the neck of my bass attach correctly to the body. What mental picture comes to mind when you hear the phrase *gang member*? While I cannot verify this, I suspect one image you have runs along these tracks. He is a heavily tattooed non-white person, possibly with a bandana on his head. He wears baggy pants and has a gun hidden in his pocket. Okay, that is fair. But what if people shim their perception of gangs to fit their racial biases? And what if white and Black people's gang activity were actually similar? Here is my reason for saying this. There is often a disconnect between people's perceptions and the historical truth in matters of race.

10. Hill, *Whiteness*, 193.

11. Clary, "Defense Pulls Pro Wrestling Into Murder Trial," line 2.

As a way to illustrate my point, let us travel back one hundred years to a time called "The Roaring Twenties." It was an era of prosperity and optimism. The sky was the limit, until the stock market crashed. That is also when white gang activity peaked. Feast or famine, the roar of the gangs went unabated on the streets of America. The fruits of their murderous lifestyles earned the gangs millions. Even when the country went broke, gangs soldiered on and continued to prosper.

Whether out of greed or need, these gangs of white hoodlums were brutal and morally deficient. One website describes how the Depression-era gangsters of the 1930s engaged in "a criminal life that included bank robberies, illegal sales of alcohol, gambling, prostitution, and black market drugs."[12] I can remember watching movies about Al Capone, John Dillinger, and others, shooting everything in sight. They killed rivals and noncompliant business owners, as well as police.

However, on movie screens, they were glorified and portrayed as heroic Robin Hood-type characters who got a raw deal from the system. And even though they were murderers, thieves, pimps, wife beaters, etc., "the public couldn't get enough of them—craving the news stories, photographs, tales of luxurious living, and the morbid facts of violent deeds."[13] The "public" clamoring for more was white America. The tradition of glamorizing white gangsters has continued. People love films such as *The Godfather*, *Goodfellas*, and *Public Enemies*.

Now let's take a look at the other side of the bookend. A government website says today's Black gangs engage in "'street crimes,' that is, serious and violent crimes (e.g., assaults, drive-by shootings, robberies, homicides) that occur on the streets."[14] Notice how similar the behaviors of yesteryears' gangs are with today's versions. But I bet I would be hard-pressed to find any reputable news agency or screenwriter portraying today's Black gang members as misunderstood heroic figures attempting to overcome their impoverished circumstances. And there are simply not many white Americans who view Black gang activity with approval, let alone admiration.

Recently, I sat in the living room of a white musician who showed me a rack full of shotguns and said, "Those gangbangers better not come after me." I knew exactly who he was referring to and what he was intimating. But in reality, the only difference between the gangs of today and yesterday is the skin color of the actors involved. It is just that the stories about them have been shimmed in such a fashion that they fit into the majority's, i.e.,

12 Alexander, "Gangsters, Mobsters & Outlaws of the 20th Century," para. 3.

13 Alexander, "Gangsters, Mobsters & Outlaws of the 20th Century," para. 6.

14. Nationalgangcenter.ojp.gov, "What is a gang?," line 5.

white, sensibilities. I hope you understand that Black gangs exist for the same reasons that the white versions of the Roaring Twenties did. That is poverty and the ostracism that follows.

Finally, many of us rely on news reports written from only one perspective to shim our attitudes about race. We may need to be more careful about the narratives we accept as factual. Put race aside, and we see the gang behavior is more similar than dissimilar. In this instance, it is identical. But our racial histories are not. Have you taken the time to consider where your beliefs about race originated? Have you examined why you hold them? A lack of historical knowledge can severely limit one's understanding about race. At that point it is easy to be misled.

SHAM

A sham is a method of falsification. As I write this a young Russian soldier is on trial for a war crime in Ukraine. What the heck is a war crime anyway? Isn't that term a redundancy? Couldn't much of what happens in war be characterized as criminal? One example occurred in a war between the French and English. According to historian Peter Ackroyd, the commander of the French garrison at Calais attempted to send a note to the king of France during a siege. The commander wrote, "We can find no more food in the town unless we eat men's flesh."[15] Unfortunately for them, the letter made its way to the English king instead of King Philip. Edward signed it and then allowed it to be delivered to the French king. That was so the French king would know who read it first. Talk about rubbing it in.

What happened next was, "In the eleventh month the women, children and old people came out from the gates [in search of food] . . . The English would not allow them to pass through their lines, and they were hounded back to the town ditch where they expired."[16] This activity is easy to classify as a crime, but few history books will. Does the refusal to let the elderly and children find food expose a malignant heart? Or is it just an example of the cruelty that occurs in war? Spin is the victor's friend, is it not? Keep in mind that many histories are written with a bias and then interpreted accordingly. Now let us look at the ethics of war a little closer and see if they are valiant or criminal.

Chivalrous behavior is defined as that which is "honorable and courteous conduct expected of a knight."[17] But Ackroyd gives us an example of

15. Ackroyd, *Foundations*, 259.

16. Ackroyd, *Foundations*, 259.

17. The Britannica Editors, "Chivalry," para. 3.

how vocabulary choices can mask evil intent. He writes that chivalry can also be "the practice whereby the laws of honor supersede those of right and justice."[18] In his example, the chivalrous knights made a pact to spare the lives of each other's royalty when they conquered a city. But they had no problem mercilessly slaughtering all of a town's women and children. Amin Maalouf cites another example of spin that swirled around the mythic English king Richard the Lionheart.

In writing about the crusade Richard led to reclaim Jerusalem, Maalouf notes, "The 33-year-old red-headed Giant who wore the English crown was the prototype of the belligerent and flighty knight whose noble ideals did little to conceal his brutality and complete lack of scruples."[19] The sham is that historians labeled this type of behavior as chivalrous, sold it to the public, and it was believed. The moral is simple: don't be quick to accept the first justification for violence against another human being. That is because a well-crafted story, such as a news report, can be a strong persuader. However, as in these examples, it can also be completely false.

SHIMMY: SHAKING ALL OVER

The shimmy is a dance where the dancers shake every part of their body. My experience with shaking differs from the shimmying of the dance. What I am referring to is the shaking that comes from fear. What do a street gang, the mafia, a political gang, the military, and racial groups have in common? Like the knights of old, they have a code of honor that may not apply to outsiders. And they use power to intimidate outsiders in some way. They can be loyal and loving to insiders, while at the same time capable of appalling behaviors toward outsiders. Biker gangs are a prime example of this. What happened to a musician friend will illustrate what I call binary ethics. Those mean that if you are an insider, then you are *really* inside. But if you ever wind up on the outside, you don't matter.

My friend, who is white, made the mistake of trying to befriend the biker gangs where he performed music. He got close, but he was never really an insider and never earned their respect. One night the bikers decided that he should share something he had, as per their insider code. When he refused, the bikers beat him to within an inch of his life. They literally danced on his head to the point of disfigurement. Knowing that white biker gangs did not like Black people, what happened to my friend scared me. So I began to carry a .38 caliber revolver to my gig every night. Here is why this is important.

18. Ackroyd, *Foundations*, 155.
19. Maalouf, *Crusades through Arab Eyes*, 209.

Dominating the outsider seems to be a consistent characteristic of every type of gang; bikers do it, mafiosi do it, and let's be honest, even racial groups do it. What follows is a time I got the shim-sham and the shimmies.

My band, Leon's Creation, was based in San Francisco. The trumpet player and I rented a small house in Santa Cruz, about eighty-five miles south of the city. We commuted to all the band's activities, but the beach made the drive worth it. Shortly after the move, the band took an engagement at a Santa Clara nightclub located halfway between our home and San Francisco. I booked the gig, making me the point of contact with the owner. I was also responsible for the band financially. One night after the bar's closing, I went to get our money, but I could not find the owner anywhere. Later I would learn he was holed up in a hotel room gambling. Being unable to locate him made me furious. In my anger I decided to do something about it. I went into his office and took what I thought was the safe containing all the night's cash. Then I headed back to Santa Cruz.

Now picture this. Once I get home I off-load the dish with a combination lock and go to bed. Around noon the next day, I get a phone call from the owner shouting every profanity imaginable at me. A few veiled threats follow before he asks me to return his property. Naturally I ask for the band's pay in return. Once he agrees to pay us, I promise to return the item later that afternoon. But as I think about it a little more, concern about what he might do to me crept in. After all, my friend's experience with the bikers is still fresh in my memory. And I know this guy would fit the description of the Roaring Twenties-type gangster mentioned earlier. As a result, my roommate and I load our guns and head to Santa Clara.

We arrive in Santa Clara, consume a couple of beers for added courage, and go into the club. Once inside we are welcomed by smiles and a lot of laughter. The owner says, "I have stiffed a lot of bands over the years, but you are the first guy with enough nerve to do something about it." My approach was rooted in the street ethos that produces the type of behavior gangs respect, violence. As it turns out, the club owner saw it that way too. I never had to buy another drink in that club from that point on. There is a funny aside to the story though. One of the reasons the owner and others were laughing when we entered the club is this: I had not taken the safe after all. What I had taken was only the safe's lock!

CHAPTER 5, PART TWO

Whiteness as Agency

ONE OF THE FREEDOMS whiteness reserves for itself is freedom from having its truths questioned. Additionally, whiteness does not allow room for challenge by Blackness. And it certainly does not allow itself to be criticized by Black people, even when using one of its icon's own words. Recently, I attended a Bible study with a white friend. On this particular night he began to extol the virtues of the Western powers during the Second World War. He believed the war was fought over freedom, and the US, together with Western Europe, standing up to Adolf Hitler. He never considered other possibilities, such as the war didn't "just happen." For argument's sake, suppose the nations that used war to colonize the Americas, Asia, and Africa, unleashed their predatory tendencies upon one another. In other words, that war happened because one country invaded another, seeking to control land and people just as in the colonial enterprises. Remember, "The person who tells one side of a story seems right until someone else comes and asks questions."[1]

While sitting silently, I knew it would have offended my friend had I said racial segregation was legal in the US during that war. That fact seems to negate part of the freedom claim. Black people had to petition the US government for the "right" to fight for the freedoms of people denying theirs. Moreover, we know who had to wait patiently for honor and recognition. And people who looked like me did not receive the same benefits as others at the war's end. The government doled out a meager amount, but it

1. Prov 18:17, New Century Version.

came slowly. For example, Black soldiers did not receive equal financial aid to restart their lives.

The idea that Black people bravely fought a war only to receive the humiliation of unfreedom is troubling. And consider this: "It was common during the Second World War for the U.S. Army to treat German Prisoners of War better than Black American soldiers."[2] This means that a white sworn enemy was valued over a Black countryman. There can be no denying this bond between enemies was forged by the agency of whiteness. Today, the same thing occurs in many other ways. That is because preferring "your kind" is considered natural in many circles. But buddying up with deadly enemies proves it isn't natural. Bonding by skin color is a choice.

THE BULLDOG'S BARK

My friend continued his monologue about the greatness of Winston Churchill. At the time, I was reading Toye's book on Churchill, nicknamed the British Bulldog. Ironically, I had just read his comments related to what was coming to light about the Kenyan occupation mentioned in a previous chapter. The comments were, "It is the power of a modern nation being used to kill savages. It is pretty terrible, . . . they're savages armed with ideas—much more difficult to deal with."[3] Churchill was correct, ideas are difficult to deal with because they become ideologies. Ideologies have consequences. This one's use led to the British controlling a people group thousands of miles away. To be fair, Churchill did say that the Africans could be conquered peacefully with "proper treatment." The role of Blackness is to repudiate such nonsense and prevent further atrocities. What follows may be even more nonsensical.

British citizens were misled into believing that the Kenyan uprisings were caused by African mental illness. Government representatives said this disorder caused Africans to be violent savages from birth. It did not enter their minds that people who had been overrun by a foreign power, then reduced to subservience, would do something about it. But, notice how the word *savage* could fly off the tongue of a respected statesman like Winston Churchill. He came of age when the press could print "the white man . . . regards [the Black] as part child, part animal, and part savage"[4] without a problem.

2. Taub, "'Are We Not American Soldiers?,'" para. 3.

3. Toye, *Churchill's Empire*, xi.

4. Olusoga, *Black and British*, 461.

Turning to Mishra once more, we find Indian and Irish people characterized as "half-child, half savage,"[5] but unlike the African, still considered human. Civil rights hero Mahatma Gandhi used "savage" to describe Black South Africans. Where did these ideas originate? A century earlier, J. G. Herder spoke of a natural law of progress. "Soon there will be European Colonies everywhere! Savages all over the world will become ripe for conversion to our culture and become good, strong, and happy just like us."[6] But Charles Darwin speculated that over time, the white civilized races would supplant the savages. In other words, Black people would eventually be wiped out by the superior races.

Why so much attention to the word *savage*? The idea of savagery, meaning lower life forms emanating from the African continent, is one of the legs that white superiority stands on. This belief system even predates Darwin. Consider something written in the fourteenth century. "Negros are in general characterized by levity, excitability, and great emotionalism. They are found eager to dance whenever they hear a melody. They are everywhere described as stupid."[7] Those words were taken from an Arab historian's take on world history. The author, Ibn Khaldun, believed the sun had baked Black people's brains, causing them to be smaller. Times have changed, right? Yes and no. The theories have changed, but the tendency to view darker-skinned people as less intelligent has not.

People who use the "it is different now" shield are probably unaware of how long these misrepresentations have circulated. A bad reputation is hard to erase. Time changes very little when it comes to race. I am old enough to remember hearing a drunk driving suspect described as a "monkey" on the evening news in the 1990s. I remember cartoons depicting President Obama as a monkey when he ran in the mid-2010s. More recently, bananas were thrown at the home of basketball superstar Lebron James in Los Angeles. Yes, racism lives on. Why so many fail to see it is baffling. Perhaps it is because many parts of the story rarely make their way into the majority culture's consciousness.

Unquestionably, racist acts are being responded to better than ever. Even so, most people do not take notice of the daily variety. More attention needs to be paid to confronting the attitudes behind racism rather than simply reacting to the latest headline-grabbing incident. My writing spotlights the challenges Black people face every day. The great African American poet Clint Smith explains why. He writes, "I'm not sure that there are days

---

5. Mishra, *Bland Fanatics*, 192.

6. Herder and Barnard, *Herder on Social and Political Culture*, 43.

7. Khaldun, *Muqaddimah*, 63.

of my life when I'm not confronted with racism. For some, that may seem hyperbolic, but it is true."[8] These words are not written about the civil rights era either. He is thirty-five years old. Many people today, especially white ones, may find Smith's words unbelievable. However, skepticism does not make them any less true. Economic discrimination and racial violence are indeed terrible elements of racism. But racism is ultimately an assault on human dignity.

JUST BECAUSE YOU DIDN'T SEE IT— DOESN'T MEAN IT DIDN'T HAPPEN

Lawyers use the words in the heading every day to argue that circumstantial evidence should be accepted as factual. What follows may seem like an unnecessary complaint by an oversensitive Black author, but it is a real-life example of how whiteness affects the daily lives of millions. One day I met a very close friend, who is white, at a restaurant. COVID restrictions were in the process of being lifted, so the place was pretty empty. The server came to the table, looked my friend squarely in the eye, and then took his order. Then she said, "And you?" But instead of looking at me, she continued to look at my friend while writing down *my* order.

She made several trips to the table to inquire about beverage refills, etc. Inexplicably, not one of those times did she ask me anything. Not one word! Every time she came to the table, she looked at my friend, and once he answered, she turned and left without so much as a glance in my direction. She followed the same pattern when it was time to pay the bill. She came to the table, handed my friend the check, turned, and left. She didn't consider that I might be paying for the meal, and I was. While placing my credit card on the table, my friend offered to get the tip. I said, no, I am not going to tip her. He pressed me a bit. I said no, her behavior towards me was despicable, and I will not reward that.

He made several attempts to get me to soften. For a split second, his persistence made me feel like I was the one being rude. Finally, I had to explain that what the server did was not just rude; it was wrong. The look on his face suggested that he felt my unwillingness to tip was me being out of line. No, this kind of treatment wears on a person, and some days I don't feel like giving in to it. When people use the term "white privilege," they do not always mean white advantage. Many times it refers to incidents like this. Since whiteness is the norm, white people are free from having to experience this type of humiliation in a public space. It just doesn't happen. That

8. Brainyquote.com, "Clint Smith."

is why my friend did not see a racial event, even though it happened right before his eyes.

The Britannica website reads, "circumstantial evidence, in law, [is] evidence not drawn from direct observation of a fact in issue."[9] Due to my friend's lack of personal experience, he witnessed my ill-treatment and missed it. Sadly, we have defined racist activity downward, making it almost impossible for anyone to be "charged" with the offense. A person must commit a heinous act that is visible and harsh to be accused of racist behavior. It is to the point that getting a conviction requires either a written record or a video of the perpetrator saying the N-word while committing the act. As long as a denial continues to result in an automatic not-guilty verdict, there is no incentive to change.

Race will not cease to be an issue if only addressed using white experiences, white vocabulary, white "truths," and only discussed on white terms. Blackness needs an equal space, an equal voice, and an equal hearing. Correspondingly, British writer Otegha Uwagba writes, "Black people cannot ourselves abolish whiteness—white people will need to relinquish it."[10] What does that mean? There needs to be an end to the presumption that white people are superior in every facet of life. I realize that may sound simplistic to you. That is valid. But as evidenced by the date of Khaldun's quote, there is no other way to reverse the historical pattern of racism that this ideology has produced than completely dismantle it. And remember, "ideology tells the world how it ought to be."[11] Considering that, what should be the role of whiteness in world affairs of the future? Let us pray that whatever it is, it does not include damaging the lives of darker-skinned people as has happened in the past.

9. Britannica.com, "Circumstantial Evidence," line 1.

10. Uwagba, Whites, 64.

11. Jenkins, Rethinking Ethnicity, 86.

CHAPTER 6, PART ONE

Blackness

THE STORY

LET US OPEN THIS chapter with a bit of Black history. During the 1960s, many Black people, Negroes as they were called, decided to discontinue the quest for white acceptance. They rejected the presuppositions that led to their inferior and subhuman designation. A white talking point emerged in response to Black discontent. Stop complaining! It was based on the idea that Black Americans have more "stuff" than their African and Caribbean counterparts, so they should be satisfied. A version of that lives on. For a recent example, last week a white owner of a professional sports team stated that if Black players do not like living here, they should go back to the suffering in Africa.

But I would ask, is having more "stuff," like a washing machine or television, a fair exchange for second-class citizenship? Then I would ask, "Would you make that trade?" It is highly doubtful that any freedom-loving white American would have said yes to either. For Christians, racism is not a concern of economics or sociology but theology. God asks us to see the best in the other *and* want the best for them. Racism does neither.

False narratives were created to ensure that when Black people raised examples of inequity or inequality, they would be written off as instances of unjustified anger. White people offer proof of racial progress by using oversimplifications, such as slavery was a problem, but we fixed it. Next up, segregation was a problem, but we solved it. Then, we gave you the right to vote, etc. However, proofs of this type may not be offered to heal racial divisions, but convince casual observers there was never much racism in the first place. Think about it: Every improvement mentioned was merely the correction of a right previously withheld. In other words, what was purported to be meaningful change was not much more than contributing the bare minimum to the process. To date, people have been allowed to exaggerate and relativize racial progress without much pushback.

Let me illustrate what I mean by using a hypothetical. Imagine it is 1845. We learn Congress is about to pass a new law. It will soon be illegal for an enslaver to kill an enslaved African without a trial. We know that for years the country's laws gave enslavers the right to treat "their property" as they pleased. Those rights included killing Africans for any reason. However, because of the outrage voiced by a few social justice-type Christians, this "right" is ending. Some would have seen ending the enslaver's right to kill as real progress. Here is the problem. They could have applauded the end of the senseless killing, but not so much as blinked an eye at the continuation of slavery. Slavery itself was the problem, not its component parts.

Try this analogy on. Baseball bats come in different weights. Let us say the average major league bat weighs thirty-six ounces. If you were beaten with a thirty-six–ounce bat every day, and then your abuser switched to a twenty-eight–ounce bat, would that be progress? Focusing on one part does nothing to address the whole. Lessening the frequency and intensity of racism is not ending it. As Mishra notes, "Racism was—and is—more than an ugly prejudice, something to be eradicated through legal and social prescription."[1] Some people will never acknowledge that racism exists in our society. They are able to dismiss the past and live in an alternate present. But how can one building block of racism be easily forgotten or overlooked? What I am talking about here is language.

Historically, white people have used words of their choosing to define Blackness. There was one catch-all term used to describe darker-skinned people that stuck. This is where the word *savage* comes into play. In keeping with European stereotypes, many viewed African people as the "antithesis of Western 'cultural superiority.' Africans were characterized in postcard representations as 'savage and uncivilized people,' an exotic other, with no cultural ownership."[2] Let us add the words *unsocialized* and *undignified* to that characterization. Generally speaking, that is what many people think rappers and Black hip-hop culture are like. Did you know the word *savage* is why we don't dance in church? More on that later.

---

1. Mishra, *Bland Fanatics*, 49.
2. loc.gov, "Africana Historic Postcard Collection," para. 5.

FROM SAVAGE TO THUG

In the American lexicon, criminal, a.k.a. thug, has replaced savage as the go-to metaphor for Black youth. The mere mention of the words *Black male* can cause discomfort for those who attach criminality to race. When I entered the ministry, the US was bogged down in "culture wars" between political conservatives and liberals. But racism has never been a conservative or liberal issue because both sides have been equal offenders. Moreover, when shared privilege is at stake, intergroup political and ideological differences seem to lose their significance.

In terms of war metaphors, Black and white conflicts are closer to comfort wars than culture wars. The presence of large numbers of Black people makes many white people uncomfortable. That is why few white people intentionally spend time where the majority of people are Black. That is not conjecture but a fact. Self-segregation would not be a reality were it not so. The "comfort wars" have left collateral damage, as you will see in the following stories. One casualty of these wars is Blackness's presumption of innocence. In the nineteenth century, Cesare Lombroso developed a theory that you could tell a criminal by the way a person looks. Matt Simon, a science journalist for Wired.com, shared this:

> Cesare Lombroso argued that you could pick a criminal out of a crowd by analyzing their features. Indeed, he argued criminals were evolutionary throwbacks, closer to apes than humans. By comparing them to "savages" around the world, you could tell if they were liable to fall into a life of crime. Just a few of the things to watch out for: "oblique eyelids, a Mongolian characteristic"; "the projection of the lower face and jaws (prognathism) found in negroes."[3]

It is easy to see why sociologist W. E. B. Du Bois could confidently state, "Nothing in the world in the United States is easier than accusing a black man of crime,"[4] a practice that continues to this day. Consider this: a white woman picked a Black teen out of a crowd and accused him of stealing her iPhone. When she confronted the kid in the lobby of an upscale New York City hotel, she tackled and assaulted him. Fortunately for the young man, bystanders intervened before the police had time to respond.

Can you imagine the first impression the officers would have finding a Black male on the floor wrestling with a white female? Be honest. It turns out she had left her phone in an Uber. The police did arrest her, but at trial,

3. Simon, "Fantastically Wrong," para. 8.
4. Azquotes.com, "W. E. B. Du Bois."

she was given probation. In doing so, the court signaled that she was entitled to be suspicious "considering . . ." To make matters worse, she would later claim she was the victim. That takes a lot of nerve!

Maybe you are thinking, "Oh, c'mon Jimi, she made an innocent mistake." Don't let that enter your mind without giving this some thought: the next time you are in the lobby of an upscale hotel, or any fancy business establishment for that matter, tackle the first teenaged stranger you find. What do you think will happen? And how would you have interpreted these facts if you were white and an adult Black man blindsided your fourteen-year-old? Would you have written it off as an innocent mistake, or turned it into another example of Black thuggishness?

Earlier this year, a Black FedEx driver named D'Monterrio Gibson was delivering packages in Brookhaven, Mississippi. A white man and his son thought he was a criminal, so they followed him and shot at him. They used a lethal weapon without any knowledge of a crime. When the Black man called 911 for help, the operator questioned him about *his* behavior. Then the police asked Gibson if he had done anything to make the white men suspicious. That is crazy! And it can be demoralizing to know your very being raises suspicion. Martin Luther King dreamed of a day when this kind of thing would no longer happen. We are still waiting.

Now let us reverse the races of the individuals involved in that scenario. Your twenty-four-year-old son works for FedEx. His route requires him to deliver packages in a predominately Black neighborhood. He is going about his regular duties in full FedEx uniform. Suddenly, a car containing two Black males gives chase and they shoot at him. Would you like to be told by the police that it was reasonable for them to be suspicious of him? Would you accept that? Here is the saddest part of all. The victim, Gibson, said, he "thought that the number of bullets fired at him was four or five, but an examination of his delivery van revealed it was more than that."[5] Yes, the Black male was a victim. And can you imagine the terror this young man experienced? If you are dismissing this story as an anomaly, don't be too quick.

My previous book *Funknology* contains a story that made national headlines. It was about a Black jogger who was chased down and killed by three white men in a Georgia suburb. Ahmaud Arbery had run past Travis and Greg McMichael's house one sunny Georgia afternoon. After seeing him run by, they armed themselves with guns, tracked him down, and killed him. The prosecutor asked the shooter, the son Travis, what he'd seen Ahmaud do that caused them to give chase. The only answer he could give was "run." The jury listened to the following comments captured on a police

5. Crown, "FedEx Reinstates Pay," para. 33.

officer's body cam while Arbery's body was bleeding out just twenty yards away: "This ain't no shuffler," the elder McMichael said of the slain 25-year-old Black man . . . this guy's an a**hole."[6] A shuffler?

When the other defendant, Roddy Bryan, was asked why he chased Arbery, he said, "Because I figured he had done something wrong."[7] So, let's investigate the "suspect," even if we aren't aware of a crime. That seems to be a conditioned response some have at the mere sight of a Black male. The focus is on the type of person, not any specific fact. Generally speaking, some people assume the worst about Blackness because it just comes naturally. It is not easy to have an equitable justice system when one group is pre-identified as the "bad guys." The three murderers in this case were not arrested for months and would have escaped prosecution entirely had a video not surfaced. Why? It was assumed they had only killed a bad guy. We will discuss what referring to a Black person as a "shuffler" connotes when we get to the dance section. Right now, let us check in on a different kind of racial misperception.

THE MILES THAT CONNECT

The following story would be kind of humorous if what it illustrated was not so common. The storyline revolved around an actual life event when the term *racist* was wrongfully applied to someone. This happens a lot. What you will find fascinating in this instance is that none of the characters looked like you might have expected. Let me introduce you to the musician who played a central role in the story, Buddy Miles. I toured, recorded, and lived with the late great African American drummer. We made music together in places as diverse as Amsterdam and Holland, to multiple tours of Texas and Louisiana. It is the state of Texas where the action in our story took place, long after both of our touring days had ended.

In April 2008 Julaine and I relocated from Boca Raton, Florida to Austin, Texas. Buddy had been living in Austin for about three years. Sadly, he passed away a few days before we arrived. During Buddy's time in Texas, he played with many of Austin's finest blues musicians. One of those musicians was an attractive white female bassist named Kim Session. Kim had been a fixture on the Austin blues scene as not only an excellent bass player but also as a promoter of shows. She decided to purchase a home south of Austin. The property was large enough to accommodate horses and other livestock. It had a picturesque view perfect for Kim to continue another

6. Klasfeld, "Greg McMichael," para. 3.

7. Maxouris, "What we learned," para. 32.

passion, officiating weddings. We will come back to Kim, the property, and the Miles connection in a moment.

The area of the Austin metroplex that Julaine and I moved to is located on the west side and is about a twenty-minute drive to town and to Kim's property. One of my closest friends in Austin was a white attorney named G. Michael Lawrence. He had a daughter, who was what many call "special needs." I intentionally chose that term out of all the ones used for that population for a reason. Samantha became a special need in our lives in more ways than being Mike's daughter. She became a true friend.

Samantha was unable to live on her own, and she lived in what is called a group home. During the day, Sam and her dorm mates attended rehabilitation centers where they could socialize and do various arts and crafts. At one point, the owner of the rehab center where Sam spent her days, who is also white, moved from our area to Kim's. Not only did she move to that area, but she moved into the property that Kim would later purchase. What follows is how Kim, the Calhouns, and the owner of the rehab center would become connected through Buddy Miles.

My first book is titled *A Story of Rhythm and Grace.* The book is part memoir and part critique of the white evangelical church regarding race issues. At the time of its release, I did not know Kim since I was not traveling in professional musician circles. I was, however, deeply involved in ministry to the differently abled community. Because of that, I became friendly with the owners and the staff at the places we frequented. Over time, I gave them signed copies of the book. The owner of Sam's rehab facility sold her home to Kim but left the book behind when she moved out. Kim found my book when she moved in. After reading the cover and seeing Buddy's name, she made an effort to track me down.

One day I got a Facebook message saying, "My name is Kim and we have a lot in common. I play bass and I was good friends with Buddy Miles." Kim and I managed to connect and discovered that we did have a lot in common. But I had no idea Kim had bought the home from the rehab owner I'll call Patsy. One day the rehab owner expressed frustration with the person who had purchased her home. According to her, she wanted to go back and get some items, but the two of them couldn't agree on a time. One day Patsy decided to show up unannounced. Now here is where it gets juicy. Patsy brought a Black male with her to lift heavy objects. When Kim denied her access because it was not a convenient time, the rehab owner assumed Kim was afraid of the Black man and told me as much.

However, when telling me the story about Kim's unwillingness to let her on the property, she had to add, "I think she is prejudiced." Those were her exact words to me, and it took a lot not to react. That is because Kim and I had become friends and I knew better. You see, part of getting to know Kim was hearing her amazing story, which is one that reveals a heart of gold. This is why. Not only was Kim a close friend to the Black drummer Buddy Miles. She was willing to invite me, a Black stranger, onto her property after only meeting me on the internet. Later on, Kim revealed that she had been married to a Black man who was legally blind! I will leave it to you to think through all the ways this story highlights the problem of how we do race.

CHAPTER 6, PART TWO

We Got the Beat(ings)

No, THIS SECTION IS not about the song made famous by The Go-Gos. Earlier, we discussed how Africans in the UK danced their way around the barriers that racism put in place. This section is about the beatings, metaphorical and physical, that have been part of the Black experience for centuries. People in the US viewed African and African American dances derisively. Notice the vocabulary used to describe negro dancing at the turn of the last century: "Men and women who dance like that have the strength for violence."[1] Attaching violence to Blackness seems to have gone on for a long time. Other Westerners believed negroes danced because of their primitive nature and underdeveloped intellect. Both groups, however, believed negroes were prone to violence, so obviously, the best way to control them was with violence.

Southern tradition held that "good boys," meaning compliant Black males, danced, and defiant ones did not. To live down to white expectations, negros began to walk in a rhythmic shuffle resembling dance steps. As hard as it might be to believe today, white people in America thought Black people walked differently due to a genetic trait. That perception was an American invention and an American export. Here is the proof. A young best-selling Black British author was aware that Black Americans were perceived to have an unusual "step" to their gait. Akala wrote in *Natives*, "People who have experienced niggerisation and lifelong racism often walk as though they are

---

1. Stearns and Stearns, *Jazz Dance*, 153.

apologizing for their existence."[2] He goes on to say that he could see that America had created a new tribe of Black people that talked, walked, and danced differently than their African and Caribbean counterparts.

Perhaps that explains why the first successful African American vaudevillian, comedian, and screen actor during the 1930s was named Stepin Fetchit. His persona was possibly based on the word "step," as in dance steps, combined with the term "bonny fetcher,"[3]—a spelling variation of the Scottish phrase "bonnie fechter." Bonny fetcher describes a very stubborn and tenacious individual. The American Fetchit was extremely popular. His popularity among white people can be attributed to being billed as the "Laziest Man in the World." The lazy Black stereotype was so ingrained into the American mind that "to step and fetch . . . described the job of a slave or handyman."[4] It is sad that stereotype has rung true to so many people for so long.

The lazy Black myth started during the slavery era. But wouldn't those who enslaved others to avoid doing the hard work better fit that description? Yet, white people convinced themselves that enslaved people were lazy. The truth is, the lazy Black stereotype was invented to justify the whippings doled out to force enslaved people to work. The threat of violence has long been a goad and guide for use in controlling Black people. Emery notes this about enslaved people in Barbados: "They undergo more fatigue . . . during their gala hours [dancing] . . . than is demanded of them in their labor."[5] Is "demanding" labor from people who did not sign up for the job logical? Are people who are not thrilled about doing that work lazy? Take a moment to fully digest the following:

> "If I don't beat them, they won't work as hard as I think they should." Enslavers complained about the laziness of their workers, but the records show that enslaved people often worked hard—and brutally so. Overseers were routinely paid commissions, which encouraged them to overwork the enslaved people. On a North Carolina plantation an overseer . . . boasted that the enslaved people had been worked "like horses." He added, "I'd rather be dead than a nigger on one of these big plantations."[6]

Ironically, the enslavers who determined how much work was possible probably did so without ever performing the tasks themselves. And

2. Akala, *Natives*, 258.

3. Olusoga, *Black and British*, 438.

4 Waywordradio.org, "Origin of Steppin' and Fetchin'," para. 1.

5. Emery, *Black Dance*, 20.

6. Stampp, *Peculiar Institution*, 85.

as historian Eric Foner points out, there was an added bonus to working the enslaved very hard. That was because "slavery for blacks was the surest guarantee of 'equality among whites,' liberating them from the low menial jobs."[7] This began early in America's history when white servants were made to feel superior to enslaved Black people. It then became beneath a white person to "work like a nigger." You only need to look at the people's skin color performing menial jobs today to see the longevity of that perspective.

Now, think through these contrasting takes on laziness by Mexican workers in Chicago. They said, "White bosses were lazy because they worked in offices and ordered other people around; African American workers were lazy because they didn't knuckle down and work hard to get ahead."[8] Really? Would it make sense for someone to work extra hard without the possibility of reward? Ever heard of the glass ceiling? The idea of glass ceilings has been described as barriers to career advancement for women in particular. But in America, "The barriers facing black employees, however, are even more acute . . . which has led many to dub promotion discrimination against them as a 'concrete ceiling.'"[9]

Let us now contrast the Mexican worker's opinions with some Black dancers held while touring California. The dancers were on a western tour, giving them a break from the segregated South. They commented that "when the show arrived in Los Angeles it was a different story . . . The people were so nasty—I guess they classed us with the Mexicans."[10] So much for racial classifications and inaccurate stereotypes.

Many people mistakenly believe our society no longer relies on stereotypes to form opinions about others. Okay, how recent does an example need to be? During a small group meeting a few weeks ago, a Latinx man said the following: "In my country's history, Chinese people replaced Africans as enslaved people because they worked harder and ate less." I sat speechless as the white attenders did not utter one word of disgust or even surprise.

But there is more to the story because in the US, Chinese people "were considered racially as well as culturally inferior. Most Americans believed that the Chinese were too different to ever assimilate successfully into American culture."[11] The first US law that involved the deportation of a specific racial group was the Chinese Expulsion Act of 1882. I'm sure millions

7. Foner, *Story of American Freedom*, 63.

8. Wade, *Race*, 182.

9. Bachman, "4 Steps Toward Demolishing the 'Concrete Ceiling,'" line 11.

10. Stearns and Stearns, *Jazz Dance*, 251.

11. Teachingresources.atlas.illinois.edu, "Chinese Experience," para. 1.

of Africans would have loved to have been deported back then. Holding unwelcome people captive is not without precedent. The Egyptian pharaoh would not allow Jewish captives to leave before God intervened. And an African cleric's story in the epilogue illustrates that this policy is still being carried out today.

Finally, take note of the way alleged racial superiority justified controlled repression. These are the words of an African woman under British "supervision" four generations after the last enslaved person left the continent. She lamented, "We would be digging a trench . . . being whipped if we worked too slowly or looked lethargic."[12] How does a person *look* lethargic? These whippings occurred in plain view of the public. What might be the sadder thing about it is those watching *knew* they had to take it. The victims had no recourse because it was the "authorities" that carried it out. If the bystanders objected, they would face the whip themselves.

In scenarios like this, the protectors of white life turn right around and become the perpetrators of violence against Black people. Should this type of behavior ever be condoned? No! That is because it sends a message to those victimized that no one cares about them or their safety. Perhaps the most troubling part happened when reports of the abuse made their way back to London. They were heard but not believed. Imagine visiting a relative's farm and falling into a well. You repeatedly cry out for help. You hear people walking by every day, you know they can hear your screams, but they choose to ignore them. Remember this, if people with the power to prevent abuse fail to do it, the abuse continues. That was true then, and it is true today.

LET THE MUSIC PLAY

I have recorded music that would be classified as rock, jazz, funk, and blues. Each one of those genres is what is also called roots music. That means the music that grew from the music maker's and hearer's lived experiences. As Jeremy Begbie writes, "Music always, to some extent, embodies social and cultural realities . . . no matter what the circumstances."[13] The circumstances enslaved Africans found themselves in, scattered across the so-called new world, were abysmal. Interestingly enough, the enslavers were unaware of the grittiness of the souls they were enslaving.

Whatever the treatment, wherever they landed, African people engaged in one activity—making music. They sang the blues to relieve their

12. Elkins, *Imperial Reckoning*, 247.
13. Begbie, *Theology, Music, and Time*, 13.

misery. They sang gospel songs hoping the God above would free them. And they sang while they worked in the fields as a means of communication between themselves. The reason was that many enslavers did not permit them to talk to each other "at work." The enslavers feared they would use the opportunity to plot rebellion rather than enrich them.

Music could not stop the beatings or the humiliation, but the music did provide the means to dance. And dance they did! Edward E. Baptist writes, "Perhaps even more on Saturday nights when the white people weren't watching—people animated by music and each other thought and acted and rediscovered themselves as truly alive, as people who mattered."[14] Think about what matters to you and makes you come alive. Identify the things in your life that give you a sense of meaning and purpose. Whatever you imagined, it was unavailable to them. They chose dance as an outlet to recall their stolen pasts.

Baptist mentions a musician who played banjo while "negroes danced."[15] But when his enslaver cut his ear off as punishment the dancing stopped. Baptist also makes note of a legendary enslaved woman named Liza Jane, who would "dance down" all the men. A song about her was sung by enslaved people on Southern plantations as an anthem of transcendence. I recorded a song with Dr. John about Little Liza Jane. Suffice it to say, our Liza Jane was free, single, and completely disengaged. The bottom line is this: It is unfortunate that Liza Jane, and those like her, were left without any other option to maintain a sense of dignity than to dance.

DO THE HARLEM SHUFFLE

The Harlem Shuffle was the name of a dance, a song, a stage play, and also part of a stereotype that led to a murderer calling his victim a "shuffler." Where did he get that term? I researched the word's origin using the Oxford and Urban dictionaries. The answers I found ranged from a type of dance, to a non-contributing person, to a dishonest person. Today, someone who deals cards can be called a shuffler.

But I want to share an amusing definition I heard on the street as a kid. A shuffler is someone too lazy to pick up their feet when they walk. This definition fits in nicely with the deeply embedded lazy Black stereotype. Putting that aside, we will now look at the first definition. That was about dancing. The dances that Black males performed in the minstrel shows of the early 1900s depicted them as the "happy, singing, dancing, funny black

---

14. Baptist, *Half Has Never Been Told*, 160.

15. Baptist, *Half Has Never Been Told*, 161.

man."[16] Maybe that is the kind of "shuffler" that Greg McMichael expected Arbery to be. Not resembling those clichés could have been one reason for his anger.

Expectations were raised when a Black musical named *Keep Shufflin'* became popular during the Roaring Twenties. One reviewer lauded it for "the tempestuous dancing for which the race is unsurpassed."[17] At that point, a Black person's shuffling was not about laziness or even dance. Black people adopted that image as a way to get along with whites. What you are about to read was written about Black dancers over one hundred years ago. I find it is still true about employment prospects for young Black males. According to the authors of *Jazz Dance,* "The negro performer found that unless he fitted himself in the mold as typical, he could get no work."[18]

From slavery days to the present, one attribute a Black person needs to gain acceptance is to be agreeable. You must smile a lot, be compliant, and never assert yourself. You are mindful that one wrong word and you could, to borrow a phrase from Uwagba, fall through the trap door of white acceptance. In times gone by, it was expected that negroes "knew their place," literally and figuratively. Dark-skinned people were not to venture beyond established social borders. The truth is, to get ahead in any profession, the gatekeepers to opportunity have to like you. But to gain broad acceptance by white people can be extra challenging when your skin color is an automatic "black mark" against you.

Oh my! Did you notice how easily the word *black* brings negativity to mind? Before we leave "Black people knowing their place," I have a question for you. Did you know that white and Black people lived in close proximity to each other when the latter's labor was free? But after the Civil War, white people claimed that living so close to Black people violated nature. That was the justification for segregation. They said God divided the races, and they were supposed to stay that way.

Whether we are willing to admit it or not, the idea of a divided species is still very much with us. Our cities are structured on that belief. We conduct much of our medical research as though the outer layer of the skin on our bodies causes internal biological differences. Despite some well-intentioned rhetoric, our thinking about race hasn't changed much over the last century. It is time for a change. Let's examine some reasons why change is so difficult.

16. Emery, *Black Dance,* 215.
17. Stearns and Stearns, *Jazz Dance,* 152.
18. Stearns and Stearns, *Jazz Dance,* 56.

ONE COLOR–MANY PEOPLES

If you were to say, "I saw a Black woman at the party," what might you be thinking? According to the Black German-American actor Zazie Beetz, "In the United States, if you're African American, it can be assumed that your family has been here for generations. In Europe, colonialism is much more alive, and it is assumed you're from Nigeria or Senegal."[19] Now consider these words from the book *Black Dance*. "In the West Indies the African was generally considered a human being, whereas in the United States slaves were frequently considered non-human."[20] They were viewed as living tools, "things," just like plows, a means to an end.

This bifurcated perception of Blackness carried over to dance. To the white observer, the West Indian style of dance was "by no means ungraceful."[21] By contrast, when American Blacks danced, whites saw the same body movements as vulgar and obscene. In fact, during that time period "a law prohibited African-Americans from dancing because it was said to be 'crossing your feet against the lord.'"[22] These are very different depictions of people of similar color dancing. How can that happen?

"Divide and conquer" is a maxim frequently attributed to Julius Caesar. In this case, the goal of this division was to get darker-skinned people to fight amongst themselves. One dictionary says, "Divide and conquer was once a very successful policy in sub-Saharan Africa."[23] The prior quotes suggest that strategy has worked well with Black people in general. However, I would like to leave you with something other than comparing the dance styles of Black people from different cultures. I am talking about a long-standing myth that African kings were just as responsible for the transatlantic slave trade as the European enslavers. To dispel that myth, I need to do two things. First, tell a personal anecdote, and then offer a quote that speaks directly to my point.

I talked with a Belizean about the morality of the US government when we lived there. Our government sent planes down to Mexico to spray the fields of farmers growing marijuana plants. He believed that to be wrong. I did not know whether or not it was done at the behest of the Mexican government, so I could not argue the right or wrong of it. All I could say was I believed they intended to keep a substance they considered detrimental to

19. Brainyquote.com, "Zazie Beetz."
20. Emery, *Black Dance*, 16.
21. Emery, *Black Dance*, 20.
22. Green, "Stereotypes," para. 6, line 4.
23. Dictionary.com, "Divide and Conquer."

the health of America's youth away from them. What I got back was something along these lines: "Just because somebody's selling doesn't mean you have to buy." That was also true of African chattel slavery.

Fast-forward twenty years, and I am discussing slavery with a white gentleman in our congregation. He did not think white people were the only ones at fault for the suffering of enslaved Africans. His reasoning was that African kings were selling their own people. Therefore they were at least partially responsible. It was a flimsy dodge from the beginning, and here is why. Akala quotes Sylviane A. Diouf as writing, "In none of the slave narratives that have survived do the formerly enslaved talk about being sold by other Africans, or by 'their own people.'"[24] This leads us back to the buyer-seller dilemma my Belizean friend and I discussed. Just because someone is selling doesn't make you innocent if you buy. And when it comes to slavery, a great guitar-playing friend used to say, "When you know wrong and do wrong, there are consequences."

The discussion about African kings also brought something else to mind. It exposes another problem with colorism. For many white people, dark skin is just dark skin, so gradations can be confusing. North African Arabs did trade in human cargo. Is there a chance the myth of Black African kings selling Black Africans began with a misunderstanding about the sellers' skin color? See the problem with dividing humanity into white and Black? In this schema, you are Black if you are darker than the one doing the seeing. It is this kind of error in perception that creates the need for a middle category. That is next . . .

24. Akala, *Natives*, 138.

CHAPTER 7, PART ONE

Shades of Grey

THE EVER-CHANGING FACE OF RACE

I AM A SIX-FOOT-TALL person of African descent. Imagine that I have walked into the Texas Department of Motor Vehicles to apply for a driver's license. When it comes time to select my race I check the white box. The person on the other side of the glass looks up, sees my Black skin, and asks if I made a mistake. To that I answer no. Then the person politely asks me to check the correct box, meaning the Black box. If I refuse, do you think this person might approve my application? I presume the answer would be a no in most cases. But what if two of my grandparents are white, and the single mom who raised me is white, what would that make me? Moreover, should I see my grandparents as members of a different race than mine? According to the US classification of races, I should.

If whiteness and Blackness are essential for accurately assigning people to their proper racial category, wouldn't it make sense for there to be a designation for people who fit neither? If we were to try, how could mixed-race people be categorized in a way that pleases everyone? That is not possible because they all fall short. In spite of that, some still make an effort. Today governments worldwide use racial classifications that are unstable at best. Since we are not to the point of doing away with the word *race*, at least we should be careful about how and why we use it.

I have titled this chapter "Shades of Grey" for two reasons. The first is to draw attention to the contradictory idea that "mixed-race" people exist. And the second is to draw attention to our society's inaccurate use of the color wheel. For example, I have walked this planet for several decades and have yet to see a completely white or an entirely Black person. Have you? And if they did exist, when they intermingle and reproduce, shouldn't those offspring be grey? Or should they be the various shades of brown we actually see? Or maybe we should adopt the verbiage British journalist Elle Hunt used when speaking of interior paint for a home, "It is not beige, it is not grey: it is greige."[1]

Despite the humor in Hunt's quip, there was a time when my peers and I used the color grey as a derogatory term for white people. The rationale went like this. You call us Black when we prefer that you call us brown—then we'll call you grey when you prefer that we call you white. When hip-hop became a cultural phenomenon embraced by white and Black, "grey boy" came to signify a white kid who acted Black (whatever that means to you). That designation continues in pop culture. There is a group of white musicians who specialize in the funk and jazz genres that are typically associated with Black musicians. They named their band the Greyboy Allstars.

The emergence of a people group situated between whiteness and Blackness has not resulted in a bridge that joins the two. On the contrary, it has caused the creation of new racial borders or the reinforcing of existing ones, as illogical as they may be. How did it come to be that the people I call "shades of grey" would need their own category? These not quite white, and not quite Black people came into existence during the time Europeans first traveled to Africa and vice-versa.

IF YOU ARE NOT WHITE, YOU ARE BLACK

The words in the heading were uttered by a "Black" Briton named Sunder Katwala during an interview. Here is why I place Black inside quotation marks. Katwala "has an Indian father and Irish mother with no black roots of which he is aware."[2] Think about that for a second. Earlier I suggested that the genesis of present-day Western society began with the British Empire. The science of anthropology became a tool in the arsenal of the colonizers and enslavers alike because it was "tied to the needs of the British Empire to understand the cultures and the groups it was seeking to rule over."[3]

There is one inherent problem with an autocratic form of government. The issue is when and how to use the power and control available to a king, dictator, emperor, or even a democratically elected official. Nowhere has

1. Hunt, "It is not beige, it is not grey."
2. Adekoya, "Biracial Britain," para. 2.
3. Brewer, *Ethnography*, 11.

that power been more abused than when assigning people to a race. That is because once that category is established, and people are assigned their place, they are restricted to them for generations.

White people's confusion and angst about mixed-race people surfaced due to the insertion of African people into "their world" during the slavery era. Robert Knox, writing in the 1850s, called the "Mulatto [mixed-race person]—a worthless race."[4] Knox added, "With the cessation of the supply of European blood, the mulatto of all shades must also cease; he cannot extend his race, for he is of no race and there is no place for him in nature."[5] These myths were created to excuse the poor treatment these unique arrivals received. Some myths function like stereotypes on steroids because of how they influence and shape worldviews. As some myths are based on partial truths, they are not all false. Yet other myths are untrue no matter how often they are repeated.

Racial mythology provided much of the motivation for the hatred aimed at these mysterious others. Those myths often skirted by unchallenged. So even without reliable data to depend on, white people believed mixed-race people were valueless. For example, *The Tragic Mulatto* is a short story about a mixed-race enslaved woman. She was the light-skinned "offspring of a white slaveholder and his black female slave . . . She believed herself to be white and free . . . [But with] her 'negro blood' discovered, she was remanded to slavery, deserted by her white lover, and died a victim of slavery."[6] This story reflects a common belief in Western society that when races mix, Black blood "cancels" white blood.

Wow! That is a little much, right? But this understanding is why Knox speculated that mixed-race people were either "receding towards the black, or advancing to the white."[7] Thus, the pinnacle of human development is "white blood." Hmm, so what matters is scoring highly on an invisible "blood color" calculator? To answer my own question, no; it is about power. This woman's story resulted from the white enslaver's right to use his property as he saw fit. Ownership privileges extended as far as the African female body. The reason that there have always been different shades of grey in Western society is that those men made full use of their power. But it was not a power evenly distributed among all white people—only the men held it.

To further illustrate the absurdity of racial and gender hierarchies, try to wrap your head around this scenario. Imagine there is a plantation

4. Knox, *Races of Men*, 81.

5. Knox, *Races of Men*, 78.

6. Pilgrim, "Tragic Mulatto Myth," para. 1.

7. Knox, *Races of Men*, 79.

located outside Macon, Georgia, owned by the Johnson family. The owners are Tom Johnson, twenty-six, and Sarah Johnson, twenty-two. When they inherited the plantation, there were fifty enslaved people living there. Due to Tom's frequent use of enslaved women's bodies, that number swelled to one hundred. All of the children "fathered" by Tom were born into slavery. Sarah was well aware of Tom's late-night escapades. As a result, she became convinced that she was not being treated equally.

What does she do about it? She decides to make herself available to some of the handsome "house servants." House servants were usually mixed-race because it was believed they were closer to a "normal human" than the darker field hand. As you might have guessed, one of her servants impregnates her. The baby is born with a chalky white complexion. The child is named Karen, and her race is listed as white to not disgrace the family name. Then the child grows up on the plantation surrounded by dozens of her enslaved cousins. Here is where it gets interesting. Karen hated "Black people"! She mistreated every one of her enslaved relatives until the day she died. Racism caused her life to epitomize the Psalm that reads, "I am a foreigner to my own family, a stranger to my own mother's children."[8]

BEYOND CONTROL

I read an article about tap dance in the US that said, "opportunities for whites and blacks to watch each other dance may have begun as early as the 1500s when enslaved Africans shipped to the West Indies."[9] As soon as the indentured Irish and enslaved Africans arrived on American soil, the two cultures exchanged many forms of music and dance. According to one article, "Both peoples took pride in skills like dancing while balancing a glass of beer or water on their heads, and stepping to intricate rhythmic patterns while singing or lilting [Irish or Scottish singing] these same rhythms."[10] Surprisingly, many dance experts believe the infamous African American shuffle and the Irish jig share a common ancestry.

A film titled *Gangs of New York*, set in 1863, "depicts blacks dancing to an Irish jig."[11] That movie demonstrates how blending dances can result in blending people. I have made my living playing funk music, a predominately Black genre. But for some reason, I am very much drawn to Celtic music. Could my affinity for Irish music be historically rooted? There is just

8. Ps 69:8, NIV.

9. Loc.gov, "Tap Dance," para. 7.

10. Loc.gov, "Tap Dance," para. 10.

11. Otto, "On the Link Between African and Irish Music," line 4.

something about funk and Celtic music that makes me want to clap my hands and stomp my feet. I can see by what the two groups experienced in early America that dance may have turned their hard times into good times. Let us fast-forward.

During the dance boom of the 1960s, opportunities for white and Black people to see each other dance became more commonplace. Before that, race-mixing at dances or anywhere else was taboo. In truth, it remains somewhat unusual today. When I began playing bass at The Tiki, funk pioneer James Brown was a megastar. He recorded a song titled "It's a Man's World." Keep in mind that many of America's founding documents expressed a similar view, providing the context for something David Northrup noted. And that was that "African presence in Europe was predominately male, as was European presence in Africa during this period [1450 to 1850]."[12] But Brown added a caveat to his "it is a man's world" proclamation. He believed the world would achieve little without "a woman or a girl." And this is when the blending of more than dance begins.

We all know what happens when young men in their twenties find themselves around beautiful females of the same age, don't we? And at this point, the ideologies of whiteness and Blackness have no control over hormones. And then unions between Black, white, and every other hued persons form naturally, just as they should. But what happens when large numbers of differently hued offspring suddenly appear in white societies? It is easy to imagine questions such as these making their way around a predominately white culture: "Who are they, and/or what are they?" As Brian Bantum writes, "Classification about bodies . . . is not only about bodies but . . . the struggle to account for difference and to control that difference."[13] At its core, racism is an attempt to control society.

During my childhood I was taught to sing, "Jesus loves the little children, all the children of the world, red and yellow, black and white, they are precious in his sight." That was at a time when Western color codes for race were being incrementally reduced. They went from five races (red, yellow, Black, white, and brown), down to four (white, brown, yellow, and Black) until eventually landing on three in the US (white, brown, and Black). Norwegian author Tony Sandset, who is of mixed-race identity, notes present-day divisions by UNESCO "still uses century-old tri-partite division of humanity into Yellow, Black, and White."[14]

---

12. Northrup, *Africa's Discovery of Europe*, 149.

13. Bantum, *Redeeming Mulatto*, 14.

14. Sandset, *Color that Matters*, 64.

Apparently, fixed racial markers can change with the passing of time. That being true, why not just use two, Black and white? Were we to do that, then everyone "in between" could be classified as a shade of grey. An alternative option would be to designate them "off-white" or "off-Black." Wouldn't that seem reasonable? Well, yes and no. I read an article about the genetic differences between white singer Taylor Swift and Black singer/rapper Kanye West (Ye). The article had a picture of two penguins beside them. Then it states that "the penguins are more different at the DNA level than our two human superstars."[15] Since a penguin's coloring is black and white, is it time to label them as mixed race? No? Then how can it possibly make sense to call people who are obviously not bicolored, mixed race?

AND YOU ARE A WHAT?

Anthony Le Donne is one of the authors of a book titled *Sacred Dissonance: The Blessing of Difference in Jewish–Christian Dialogue*. Le Donne is of Italian descent but is often mistaken for Black because of his darker than what some have purported to be a "normal" skin tone. Speaking of the racial dissonance his appearance creates, Le Donne writes, "I have occupied many borders in my life . . . My daughter once wrote in a third-grade assignment that her daddy was 'a black."[16] Then he adds, "At the time, however, I was presented a problem . . . Do I really want my eight-year-old daughter to know that I don't think I'm black?"[17] Presumably thinking that would signal there is something negative about being Black. He then concludes, "After a great deal of struggle within the borderland between black and white, I decided to be definitely grey."[18]

His daughter is not the only one to reach the checkpoint at the border of Black and white and find they are required to make a choice they should not have needed to make. I have a daughter, and her mother is white. My parents warned me that the borders between white and Black were hard and fast in America. And these borders have maintained white racial purity and privilege. My parents repeatedly said that children born to "interracial" unions would have problems. I did what many of us do today when confronted with racial issues. I convinced myself that we had moved past that. I assured myself that their concern was a generational thing and my daughter would be fine.

15. Jarry, "Are You There, Race?," para. 10.

16. Le Donne and Behrendt, *Sacred Dissonance*, 50.

17. Le Donne and Behrendt, *Sacred Dissonance*, 51.

18. Le Donne and Behrendt, *Sacred Dissonance*, 51.

Not so fast. I may have moved past judging mixed-race unions. And some of my friends may have moved past it as well. But most people in my daughter's world, socially and professionally, had not. I was very disheart-ened when I looked at one of her promotional bios to find she had opted to identify as Latina. It said to me she couldn't be white, and she couldn't be Black, and so she settled on what was an "allowable identity." I was both sad and mad that our society forced her to identify as something other than a person.

One point that needs emphasizing is that even when you do not fit the norm, you can't escape being defined by it. In our culture, people frequently use skin color to define and not describe. Consider the following hypotheti-cal as one example. One afternoon you are driving home from work. You see a kid break her leg in a fall and help her. When you get home, you tell your partner, "I am late because I helped a Black kid who'd fallen off her bike." What did her skin color have to do with her broken leg? Nothing! This happens all the time.

Now let us consider another example. South African celebrity Trevor Noah, who we would categorize as "mixed race" in the US, says this about his birth: "When the doctors . . . reached in and pulled out a half-white and half-black child who violated a number of laws, statutes, and regulations—I was born a crime."[19] He writes that when the authorities asked his mother for the father's name, she made one up because "under apartheid, the gov-ernment labeled everything on your birth certificate: race, tribe and nation-ality. Everything had to be categorized."[20] If you think that was South Africa, and it was different there, it wasn't.

Malla Nunn, a green-eyed, mixed-race author, describes what be-ing categorized as "non-white" was like in Swaziland, about five-hundred miles north of South Africa. "Having to be 'coloured,' as we were called then, isolated us and, in many cases, taught us to disdain the black part of ourselves."[21] I know of several instances here in the US when white mothers declined to place a Black father's name on a child's birth certificate. Not because it was illegal, but if the father was "unknown" or not present, there was a possibility they would place the child in the white category. Then she or he would avoid the difficulties that Nunn describes.

Noah wrote that one way South Africans avoided those difficulties was to smuggle the kids out of the country because "being a mixed-race family

---

19. Noah, *Born a Crime*, 26.

20. Noah, *Born a Crime*, 27.

21. Nunn, "I Grew Up Mixed-Race in Southern Africa," para. 5, line 4.

under apartheid was . . . unbearable."[22] Unbearable is a fitting description. If you are one to use the shield of "we all have problems," don't. Because if you are white, whatever problems you have do not include having your basic humanity questioned daily. The online media outlet *Vox* published an article about the impact mixed-race categories have on one's self-image. It reads, "Studies illustrate a group of people who struggle with questions of identity and where to fit in, often feeling external pressures to 'choose' a side. There's evidence that mixed-race people have higher rates of mental health issues and substance abuse, too."[23] These categories debase the dignity of the individual. Let's reverse that starting now.

22. Noah, *Born a Crime*, 28.

23. Vox First Person, "Loneliness of being mixed race in America," para. 4.

CHAPTER 7, PART TWO

Why Am I Here?

Do you remember the Wutzit and The Rock-A-Teens from the first chapter? That was the beginning of my excursions into white middle-class society. The reality is that those trips, in combination with friendships with white kids named Brad, Mike, Jim, Joe, Dave, and Don at Lincoln High school, set the course for the rest of my life. Early on, my parents taught me that hard work and determination could lead to anything I wanted. My problem was that until I made those trips across the border, my imagination was limited to excelling at sports or winning fights. That path would have ended with me doing manual labor at either Lockheed, Ford, or some such. There is nothing at all wrong with those jobs. I am just saying that is what I saw the older kids doing in my neighborhood. And so that was the path I would have followed had I not been willing to cross a border. By the way, the key word in the last sentence is *willing*, not *crossing* or *border*.

Through my border-crossing experience, I learned that location, location, location has a much broader application than a real estate slogan. Because of that, I made sure my daughter went to school in upscale areas before attending a private school. I wanted her vision of what is possible in life to be grounded in more than good advice from me. And I wanted the world that she was living in to confirm it. Consider this: "Much of the contemporary research on inequality emphasizes the experiences of people after adulthood."[1] But most people have a good idea about their place in the world long before adulthood. If society forces you to be a shade of grey,

1. Christerson et al., *Growing up in America*, 2.

that adds one more step to the process. At that point, the question becomes, which part of me fits into what place? That is tough!

Earlier I used the phrase "life's lottery" for a reason. Remember, there have always been a small number of Black, white, mixed-race people who win life's lottery and become successful in various fields. It is easy to point to the relatively small number of darker-skinned success stories and discount much of what I write by saying, "Look, they made it." If you are inclined to think that way, you might want to consider the following: lottery commercials platform the grand prize winner attempting to convince the viewer that they have a good chance to be that person. That is a way of pointing to an infrequent success story as being the norm too.

What those commercials fail to mention is that most people who buy tickets don't win anything. The same holds true for millions of darker-skinned people stuck on the lower rungs of the occupational ladder. The odds of them winning aren't very good. That is because skin color continues to impact a person's overall chances in life. A lottery is a game of chance, but life isn't. I hate to hear people say, "He happens to be African American," as though my mom grabbed a lottery ticket at the hospital's reception desk when I was born. Social positioning tied to race is not blind luck, and it results from choices people make with eyes wide open.

Some not-so-positive events in my home state illustrate this point. An article written for the Federal Reserve Bank of Texas about post-COVID employment reads, "Black unemployment rates have spiked much more than white jobless rates during recessions."[2] Race makes life's playing fields different. No matter how much resolve a person may have, being told "no" often enough is demoralizing. Additionally, it is illogical to characterize those you are unwilling to socialize with, live by, or hire, as people who don't want to work without firsthand knowledge. Please consider this: Your imagination may not be accurate about the opportunities darker-skinned people have.

RACIAL COGNITIVE DISSONANCE

Many ethnicities that were once considered something other than white are now being awarded white status regardless of physical appearance. Ever-changing census designations buttress this point. But a change in census designation does not automatically translate to equal social status. Trevor Noah lamented in his autobiography that as a mixed-race South African, he had a chance to be "elevated" to white status and enjoy the attached benefits.

2. Jones and Tracy, "Black Workers at Risk," line 4.

That was until Nelson Mandela took power and ruined everything by changing racial classifications. Where is your racial borderline? "I don't have one" is not acceptable because in America, we all do. But it can get confusing.

Borderlines aren't quite as perceptible as they once were. Just today, I listened to a commentator's remarks about a verdict in a high-profile court case. What follows is a description of the jury's demeanor as they enter the courtroom. The reporter said, "I don't know, juror number seven looks as if he is white, and he had a stern look on his face." He looks as if he is white? Is it possible to look white and not be white? At this point it becomes a matter of optics, meaning vision and perception, followed by interpretation. Many people have difficulty resolving the internal conflict that different shades of grey bring. They are incapable of defining what they see, so they categorize a mixed-race person as "obviously different." When people lack the mental framework necessary to create a different category for themselves, it leads to "racial cognitive dissonance."

Cognitive dissonance means "the state of having inconsistent thoughts, beliefs, or attitudes."[3] We tend to view mixed races inconsistently, don't we? One problem with seeing the world in Black and white is overlooking important details about a person. I worked at a church where one of the staff was from Egypt. He had an olive complexion and wore his curly hair in an Afro style. He was the music director, making him one of the first people a person sees upon entering for worship. One morning an attender walks in, looks at the stage, and asks where the Black guy is. This pastor is married to a white woman, his children are considered white, and he is culturally white (again, whatever that means to you). He would have been surprised and possibly offended had he been told someone in the congregation saw him as Black.

Let us look at a potential problem that could arise from that misperception. What if most of the people in the congregation saw my friend as white, but this sole congregant didn't? Now imagine that my colleague was in distress in a mall parking lot encircled by several white shoppers. That congregant spots him and attempts to help by calling the local emergency line. The 911 operator asks for a description of the distressed person. The congregant says he is a Black male about six feet tall. The EMS team shows up and circles the parking lot several times. Since my friend is not Black, at least according to their definition, they drive off.

---

3. Lexico.com, "Cognitive dissonance."

COGNITIVE ILLUSIONS–WE
SEE WHAT WE BELIEVE

We are about to begin the religion section, and the one we will look at first is Judaism. In anticipation of this I need to mention an interesting fact. At different times the Jewish people have been viewed as a nationality, a race or ethnicity, and a religious group. We should take note of something else that is true about the way some characterize Jewish people. Some say the Jewish people are obstinate and arrogant. That stereotype began when they refused to join the Roman conquerors in worshipping their gods, even at the risk of execution. According to scholar Mary C. Boys, even the influential Christian reformer Martin Luther voiced a similar idea.

According to Boys, "Luther saw the Jews as the enemies of society; a Christian society had no room for dissenters."[4] I like to frame these "facts" in a much more positive light. When confronted with unpleasant options, Jewish people remained faithful to their calling—despite external pressure to do otherwise. That quality is not only admirable, it is worth emulating. Unfortunately, this would lead to an increase in Western antisemitism. In fact, as I write this, many people believe there to be a rise in that very thing.

As we saw with whiteness and Blackness, faithfulness to one thing can be construed as a rejection of another. It was that kind of thinking that led to religious Jews being viewed as insular and standoffish. People can portray them as outsiders, as has happened many times in the past. It is an easy thing to conjure up hate-filled stories about an outsider. Boys informs us that one Catholic scholar claimed that "the Talmud explicitly commanded Jews to kill Christian women and children."[5] The English once labeled Jewish people criminals and forced them to wear badges. Sound familiar? Remember, skin color functions as a badge for people stereotyped as criminals today. Ironically, the Spanish accused Jewish people of causing the "black plague."

It saddens me that Jewish people have found themselves in a lose-lose situation throughout history. Boys notes that when Jewish people suppressed some aspects of their religion to fit in, they "became even more vulnerable to malign prejudice in post-Enlightenment European nation-states."[6] And when they attempted to assimilate into Western European culture, they ran into the Nazi horror. Defaming a perceived enemy is an old practice that has not gone away. And Jewish people are not alone in having stories made up

4. Boys, *Has God Only One Blessing?*, 68.

5. Boys, *Has God Only One Blessing?*, 70.

6. Mishra, *Bland Fanatics*, 42.

about them to justify disapproval. Since the murder of George Floyd, some white Christians claim Black people are committed to killing police officers.

As outrageous as those claims have been, many believe them to various degrees. The reason people can misread the intentions of Jewish and Black people is simple. Those prone to believe these stories have never spent quality time with large numbers of people from either group. They only share what they hear inside their own social network. In a court of law, repeating what others tell you as fact is called hearsay evidence. Guess what? The courts reject that form of evidence, and so should you. You should get to know a large number of people in the group you accuse of killing women, children, and police officers before buying into that kind of rhetoric. By the way, if you happen to run across someone bent on killing anyone, report them. If you are not personally aware of someone contemplating murder, avoid spreading hearsay information.

Black and Jewish Americans forged a strong bond during the civil rights era. Each group cared about the plight of the other. Jewish people marched and died for the rights of Black people to be recognized. And Black people vigorously supported efforts to keep the memory of the Holocaust alive. These two peoples were like-minded concerning several issues. But with the passing of time all of that changed. Karen Brodkin wrote openly about how Jewish whiteness became American whiteness. This means that Jewish social identity was placed in contrast with American Blackness. This "whitening" of the Jewish people diluted the relationship that had developed between the two marginalized groups following the Holocaust.

This is how changes of that kind play out in everyday life. I remember having a conversation with one of my closest friends, Rudy. He is Jewish, and one day he casually mentioned that he is white. That triggered a memory of another conversation I had decades earlier with a guitarist who was a light-skinned Ashkenazi Jew. I told him that he could not understand racism because he was white. He corrected me, saying he was not white but Jewish. He also let me know he had faced racism many times. Jazz music critic Nat Hentoff writes of his own "not-white but Jewish" experience this way, "As a child in Boston . . . it was foolish of me to go out alone after dark and become prey to violent roving bands of [white] Christian youngsters whose most satisfying sport was to break the faces of Jews."[7]

Just think, those young thugs engaged in reprehensible activities against someone they believed to be one of "those people." They did this unaware that in a few short years, "those people" would become "our people." See how painless inviting others in can be? Life lesson: Those on the outside

---

7. Hentoff, *Nat Hentoff Reader*, 232.

today might be inside tomorrow. This is why you should not get too hung up on your dislike for them, no matter who they are. That being the case, it is vital that everyone clearly understands what a race is and what it is not. Do you know? Have you given it much thought? Or have you just rolled through life thinking race is something "everybody knows"?

In my lifetime, I have watched my Jewish friends, such as my guitar-playing friend, Latinx friends, and others, become "white." They were able to assimilate into mainstream American life without any change in their appearance. Sandset suggests that in our Western racial drama, "Skin in a way becomes culture."[8] Please remember that we are not living in a post-racial world. That means "at its visual, everyday level: the reading of skin"[9] *is* what decides where one belongs and with whom. The word *assimilate* means to incorporate into something. And one of the words that the dictionary lists as an antonym of *assimilate* is *conflict*. To paraphrase the words of Jewish philosopher Martin Buber, the only way to end conflict is to acknowledge the truth. That truth is this: It is time to embrace the unique identities of mixed-race people and fully accept them as they are.

8. Sandset, *Color that Matters*, 155.

9. Sandset, *Color that Matters*, 159.

SECTION THREE

Religion

"Whatever you do in life, do it with love."

—JIMI CALHOUN

CHAPTER 8, PART ONE

Judaism

MOSES LISTENED

WE ENDED THE LAST section discussing Jewish ethnic identity in the US. This chapter will begin with a discussion about Jewish identity in general. *The Gift of the Jews* is a book by Thomas Cahill that I liked very much, not because of the theology but its premise. Here, it is the subtitle that is important. Its basic claim is that this tribe of desert nomads changed the way we all live. In the book, Cahill takes his readers on a journey through the Hebrew Scriptures to show how this small tribe has impacted Western society like no other.

The book opens with this line: "The Jews started it all—and by 'it' I mean so many of the things we care about, the underlying values that make all of us, Jew and gentile, believer and atheist, tick."[1] Today the number of Jewish people worldwide is about fifteen million. That they still contribute positively to society in disproportionate numbers is not debatable. But the Jewish people did even more for Christians and Muslims. They introduced us to God. This is what I mean. God would not be known to us without them. But there is more.

When you hear someone say they are Jewish, what do they mean? Could they be saying they are a people like Ethiopians? Are they identifying as an ethnicity like Sicilian? Would they be speaking of their nationality like a Bolivian? Maybe they are informing you of a religious affiliation, like an Anglican. They could mean one or all. Despite having this much diversity

1. Cahill, *Gift of the Jews*, 3.

within "Jewishness," they are a family. For example, "85% of U.S. Jews say they feel at least 'some' sense of belonging to the Jewish people, including roughly half who feel 'a great deal' of belonging (48%). And eight-in-ten say they feel at least some responsibility to help fellow Jews in need around the world, including 28% who feel 'a great deal' of responsibility."[2]

Having a sense of responsibility is a fundamental value of Judaism. In this chapter, I will take it one step further. I am arguing that Judaism itself is a religion of responsibility. Rabbi Jonathan Sacks says, "The definition of a Jew is one who sees the problems in the world and seeks to fix them. Judaism is God's call to responsibility and to be a Jew is to accept responsibility."[3] As Sacks implies in his writings, they are also responsible for, and linked to, all humanity. Here is why.

Jewish ethical codes emphasize basic obligations to others, which results in a need to prioritize self-interests. In many instances, the people function "as a 'single body' and a 'single soul' moved by one another's pain."[4] That is the opposite of the "what's-in-it-for-me" mindset that dominates much of the Western worldview. I will share more about that later. For now, let me ask you to think about this: Many people believe being considerate of others is the key to happiness. To paraphrase Hillel, "Whatever it is you don't like done to you, don't do that to somebody else." That is also a sure way to prevent conflict.

Unfortunately, people do not always act as they should. We saw that with the mixed-race situations in the previous chapter. Why? US racial categories play a part. As it relates to Jewish people, immigration policies factor in. For example, during the Second World War the US refused asylum to thousands of Ashkenazi, or white, Jews fleeing Europe. Despite that, most Ashkenazi Jews here identify as white Americans. Jewish ethics compels them to overlook the reason entry was denied, racism. Please keep this in mind. The concept of ethics includes attitudes and motivations as well as the behaviors of people.

To switch gears, there is one term in a Pew Research study that touched my funny bone, "Jews in all hues."[5] Yes, this is a serious book about serious matters. But since my stance is that there is only one race, I was able to crack a smile. Jewish scholar Mijal Bitton sees "a growing gap between how mainstream Ashkenazi Jewish communal organizations think of Jews of color."[6] Jews of color? What does she mean? Let us see by returning to more serious content.

2. Pewresearch.org, "Jewish community and connectedness," para. 3.

3. Sacks, "Way of Responsibility," line 3.

4. Sacks, *To Heal a Fractured World*, 94.

5. Pewresearch.org, "Race, ethnicity, heritage," para. 26.

6. Pewresearch.org, "Race, ethnicity, heritage," para. 40.

For starters, there are a variety of Jewish people groups with names like Ashkenazi, Sephardi, Mizrahi, and Ethiopian. And they are not monochromatic. Like the shades of grey described in the previous section, Jewish skin colors range from very light to very dark. That said, take note of this plea in the Song of Songs: "Dark I am . . . Do not stare at me because I am dark."[7] One commentator interprets the second part to mean don't look down on me because I am dark. Why is maligning dark skin tone so common? Why can't this habit be broken? To me, it is a spiritual problem. It is a matter of the heart and not the mind.

Perhaps some of you are learning for the first time that there are darker-skinned Jews out there. Some of these darker-skinned Jews are part of the people group that resisted being swallowed up by Western colonialism in Ethiopia. As discussed earlier, an Ethiopian often asks this question when meeting someone for the first time: "Who are your people?" Former Israeli prime minister Shimon Peres tells us how it should be. He said, "We [Jews] are one people, tied to an ancient and splendid faith, and no physical force and no external difference can divide us. For we are one people, there are no black and white Jews: there are Jews. History and faith bind us together forever."[8] That does get to the heart of the matter.

MY RABBI

Rabbi Sacks has had an enormous impact on my spiritual life. Between 1991 and 2013, he was chief rabbi of the largest Orthodox body in the UK. He left us on November 7, 2020. Sadly, I never had the opportunity to meet him. Despite that, he has taught me much about Judaism, the Jewish people, and life. Rabbis Sacks makes an observation that is relevant to this entire section. He writes, "The relationship between Judaism, Christianity, and Islam, has historically been a poisoned one, I seek to understand why."[9] One of the questions for us is this: If I am a Christian, am I willing to reexamine my attitude towards the other Abrahamic faith traditions? The truth is, Judaism, Christianity, and Islam share many similarities. However, suspicion, and even conflict, frequently mar their interaction. That is a shame. Is it time to change that?

I believe Christians should listen to the views of people from other faiths. That is because "wisdom, understanding and knowledge exist in

---

7. Song 1:6, NIV.

8. Naim, *Saving the Lost Tribe*, xiii.

9. Sacks, *Not in God's Name*, 23.

everything."[10] And there is a reason why that is true. Think this through. Regardless of how sophisticated general knowledge is, it exists because God gifts it equally. You realize we have geniuses who are atheists, right? You see, every human being has something to offer. Not because of what they believe, but because of who God is. We should never feel superior or inferior to anyone.

Psalm 23 begins, "The Lord is my shepherd."[11] That passage is familiar to Jews, Christians, and some Muslims. When Rabbi Sacks wanted to highlight the Jewish people's love for debate, he did so with humor. He modified the Psalm to say, "'The Lord is our shepherd,' but no Jew is ever a sheep."[12] He did this to emphasize one beautiful trait of Jewish people. They are not "sheepish" and can hold strong opinions while engaging in loving dialogue. We must understand all of what that joke has to say to us. Why? Because this type of dialogue is crucial if we are to overcome race issues and national and religious pride. Rabbi Sacks quotes William James as saying, "Wisdom . . . is learning to overlook."[13] I would add that looking past discord is a vital piece as well. Let us see how looking past conflict plays out in two real-life examples.

SHARING LIFE BEFORE SHARING BELIEFS

Remember my Jewish friend Rudy? I met him during my marathon running days when we both lived in Manhattan Beach, California. We ran eight miles along the beach five days a week together. Weekends were different because we could run eighteen to twenty-four miles in the mountains. What would you imagine we did during those long runs besides breathing heavily? Argue! That is right, we could argue almost the entire way. It didn't matter if others were present, and many times there were. It was difficult for our friends to comprehend how we could have such long and heated debates while remaining very close friends.

Allow me to share why. There are not many people on the planet I can say I love more than Rudy Greene. Despite being smarter than me, he was never condescending or impolite. And he did not make our disagreements personal. Our debates were similar to how the rabbis would resolve conflict through a process called Machloket l'Shem Shemayim. That translates to arguing for the sake of heaven, a.k.a. constructive conflict. As the Institute of Jewish Studies

10. Dan, *Teachings of Hasidism*, 41.

11. Ps 23:1, NIV.

12. Green, "Prof. Alex Green Interviews Rabbi Jonathan Sacks," para. 17.

13. Sacks, *Home We Build Together*, 194.

website puts it, "One can engage in machloket in a destructive way resulting in a damaged relationship. Or, one can engage in machloket in a constructive way, where the relationship is preserved."[14] That requires developing the skill to love those who hold strong opinions that differ from yours.

The following anecdotal evidence is drawn from my experience as a professional bassist. I will use these illustrations to show the difference between covenantal and contractual relationships. There were three ways a bassist could earn a living. You could be a touring pro and contract your services to the highest bidder. Those are the musicians you see performing with your favorite singer in concert. They are usually called "the backup band." The Four Tops hired me on the spot as that kind of musician to finish out a tour. I did not see or hear from them for twenty-five years once the tour was over. That illustrates the amount of loyalty involved.

Then there was the recording musician. That position is similar to a touring pro in that you contract your services. However, you perform in a recording studio rather than playing live on stage. Then you get paid and go home. You can perform your parts without the artist being present. Even though your name will be on the record, you may never meet the singer. In this wing of the business, the music is created on a purely transactional basis. For example, I play notes, and you pay me. There is no loyalty involved beyond what is stated in the contract.

Musicians in self-contained bands like U2 or The Rolling Stones operate differently. That is because they are the main personnel. They are not paid by the note, and everyone has a stake in the outcome. Additionally, being an equal member ensures each player has creative input. When disagreements occur, all parties are committed to working through them. That is how my band Creation functioned. Rather than contracting to perform bass parts for an agreed upon amount of money, I committed to making music with one group of people. That commitment was firm regardless of any financial concerns or problems that might surface.

My involvement with Creation was covenantal. My relationship with other band members would not allow me to void the agreement because of any external circumstance. And I didn't. I could have made more money in other settings. I could have done higher profile tours as a contracted musician, but I chose not to. A famous adage attributed to Thomas Aquinas says, "What a person loves tells you who they are." Said another way, people pursue what is important to them. Living in community has always been important to me. A covenantal relationship is built on mutual trust, which is its own reward. A contractual relationship is different. It is grounded in

---

14. Chabad.org, "What is Machloket l'Shem Shamayim?," para. 3.

the individual needs of two parties seeking mutual benefit. However, life is dynamic, and contracts cannot account for all of its changes. That is why contracts are broken. One the other hand, a covenant is a bond and is therefore enforceable in the face of every obstacle.

The covenantal arrangement just mentioned mirrors the Jewish people's relationship with God. Put simply, God formed a band, and the people of Israel agreed to join. Rabbi Emil Fackenheim makes two observations about the covenant religious Jews and Christians share. He suggests that the Jewish people are born into this covenant, and baptism is the means of entering it for Christians. Please know the rabbi is speaking in general terms. He is aware Christians come to faith in different ways. That does, however, echo what Paul says about Gentiles being grafted into Israel's promise. As Franz Rosenzweig writes, "Before God, then, Jews and Christians both labor at the same tasks. He can dispense with neither."[15]

FORMING A COVENANT

Judaism was born with these words: "I will establish my covenant as an everlasting covenant between me and you and your descendants after you for the generations to come, to be your God and the God of your descendants after you."[16] The purpose of the covenant is stated in Genesis 12, where it reads, "all peoples will be blessed through you."[17] This is the covenant God made with one man that extends far beyond him. And it not only reveals Jewish mission, but also Christian mission. So it is not just about you when it comes to being in relationship with God. Having a genuine concern for the well-being of others *is* part of a Christian's personal relationship with God.

Are you living as if racial injustice does not exist, and if it does, it is not your problem? If so, consider this: "Do not stand idly by when your neighbor's life is threatened [or taken]."[18] We are to be people of action and not apathy, and this is why. We often hear the question asked, "Why does God allow so much pain and suffering in the world?" It just may be that it is allowed to give us a job to do. That leads us to a better question. Why do *we* allow so much pain and suffering to exist in the world, and stand idly by as it happens?

Individualism is the main enemy of religious all-inclusiveness in Western culture. Buber says we see ourselves as one type of "thing" among many

15. Rosenzweig, *Star of Redemption*, 415.

16. Gen 17:17, NIV.

17. Gen 12:3, NIV.

18. Lev 19:16, New Living Translation.

other things. We are an atomistic society "existing or operating separately from other similar things or people."[19] The result is that we see humanity as a collection of autonomous "selves." The spirit of religious individualism leads many to ignore other "selves" as long as they don't threaten their happiness.

How soullessly can one live? That should not be faith's legacy. As Rabbis Sacks writes, "the world has changed. Relationships have gone global. Our destinies are interlinked."[20] What is the rabbi saying? As a result of Moses' listening, Jews, Christians, and Muslims can share in God's inexhaustible love together. And because Moses listened, we have an obligation to try.

How did Moses listen? When God called, Moses immediately responded, "Here I am."[21] Rabbi Joseph Soloveitchik explains the importance of that action. He writes, "In the case of Moses . . . [God] tells Moses if he accepts the mission, if he accepts the task of redeemer everything will be all right; not everything will be wasted."[22] Once Moses understood what that meant, he "expressed his willingness to sacrifice himself for the sake of the people."[23] Paul reminds us that Christians are to follow suit, writing, "Do nothing out of selfish ambition . . . Rather, in humility value others above yourselves, not looking to your own interests but each of you to the interests of the others."[24]

I have heard it said, "An apple doesn't fall far from the tree." But I would add this: that is true until someone moves it. And that is what we have done with the Christian faith. We have moved it away from our tree, Judaism. It has been written that "Judaism is the fire and Christianity the rays."[25] One definition for fire is, "to give life or energy to"[26] something. Google *ray*, and you'll find it defined as a "luminous body." We see from the definitions that Christians and Jews are both called to be lights to the world. But, when there is conflict between the two, the fire loses its energy. Then the rays lose their brightness, and not much light shines as a result. A good place for Jews and Christians to rekindle the fire again is through joint participation in Tikkun Olam, i.e., "repairing [the] world," making the world a better place through volunteering, social justice work, and philanthropy.[27]

19. Dictionary.Cambridge.org, "Atomistic."

20. Sacks, *Not in God's Name*, 103.

21. Exod 3:4, NIV.

22. Soloveitchik, *Visions and Leadership*, 90.

23. Soloveitchik, *Visions and Leadership*, 90.

24. Phil 2: 3–4, NIV.

25. Fackenheim, *To Mend the World*, 79.

26. Britannica.com, "Fire."

27. Jel.jewish-languages.org, "Tikkun Olam."

CHAPTER 8, PART TWO

Tikkun Olam: The Covenant in Action

THE IDEA OF TIKKUN Olam is an extension of the mandate to bless others found in the Abrahamic covenant. In his book *Visions and Leadership*, Rabbi Soloveitchik draws a contrast between the characteristics of individualism and covenantal life. Covenantal traits are "sacrificial action, the ability to give away and to renounce basic inalienable rights . . . for the benefit of another human being or community."[1] The rabbi cites Abraham as an example of someone with great wealth but willing to give it all away for a greater vision.

Jesus said that as Christians we are to let our "light shine before others, that they may *see your good deeds*."[2] Isaiah says this about the Jewish people: "Nations will come to your light, and kings to the brightness of your dawn."[3] It should be self-evident that observant Jews and Christians are to participate in tangible and visible actions that bring healing to the world. I will not speculate about what prevents some Jewish people from jumping in. But I do know why many Christians are not that keen on the idea, apathy. But there is hope. What follows are three examples of what Rabbi Sacks means when he suggests that the person of faith sees the problems in the world and takes action to remedy them. As these examples illustrate, there

1. Soloveitchik, *Visions and Leadership*, 42.

2. Matt 5:16, NIV.

3. Isa 60:3, NIV.

is potential for reversing the detrimental effect that the atomistic worldview has on social action.

SCHINDLER'S LIST

The 1994 film *Schindler's List* was a great movie but a better story. The storyline demonstrates Tikkun Olam because the lead character stretches himself for the good of another. In this instance, it was not the Jewish people engaged in Tikkun Olam: they were the recipients. You might remember the story. Oskar Schindler persuaded Nazi officials to have Jewish people that were scheduled to be "exterminated" work in his factory. Schindler was far from the typical humanitarian. He was said to have been a drunk, a womanizer with a gambling addiction. He was also a member of the Nazi Party. But, despite all of that, he risked his life to save the lives of hundreds of Jewish people during the Second World War.

In the Iona Community we recite a prayer that says, "We will not offer to God that which costs us nothing." As a community we want to stretch ourselves, and be stretched, in hopes of bringing justice and peace to the world. Shortcomings aside, that is what Oskar Schindler did. And those actions reflect the essence of Tikkun Olam. This is the outcome of a life lived on the edge.

> In 1949 they [Oskar and wife Svitavy] settled in Argentina with several of the Jewish families they had saved. Having spent the bulk of his profiteering fortune on bribes, Schindler unsuccessfully attempted to farm. He went bankrupt in 1957, and the next year he traveled alone to West Germany, where he made an abortive entry into the cement business. Schindler spent the rest of his life supported by donations from the Schindlerjuden ["Schindler Jews," as they called themselves]. He was named a Righteous Gentile by Yad Vashem in 1962 and was interred in the Catholic cemetery on Mount Zion in Jerusalem.[4]

Inconsistency and controversy were the hallmarks of Oskar Schindler's life. He only moved to South America because he was wanted for war crimes back home. Author Aron Hirt-Manheimer said, "For the record, the real Oskar Schindler was no saint, and the 1,200 Jews he saved were not sheep. In fact, in a reversal of roles, during the final days of the war, a group of Schindlerjuden . . . took direct action to save Schindler's life."[5] The movie

4. Pallardy, "Oskar Schindler," para. 6.
5. Hirt-Manheimer, "Schindler's List," line 13.

portrayal was one of a hard-nosed opportunist with a soft side. Whatever the real story was, at least twelve hundred Jewish people were spared extinction by a Roman Catholic man. Tikkun Olam is for the good of the world more than the advancement of any one cause.

JOHN RANKIN–UNDERGROUND RAILROAD

John Rankin was a Presbyterian minister and a participant in the Underground Railroad. That "railroad" was not made up of trains exclusively. It was a network of people helping enslaved Africans escape captivity. The people involved provided transportation to the north any way they could. One history website says, "In the deep South, the Fugitive Slave Act of 1793 made capturing escaped enslaved people a lucrative business, and there were fewer hiding places for them."[6]

It was illegal for a white person to help an enslaved person escape. In fact, there were fines, jail sentences, and public ostracism attached if one was caught. Despite this, Rankin "opened his home to African Americans seeking freedom. . . . He kept the runaways hidden until it was safe for them to travel further north."[7] Why did Rankin do it? The following words reveal why. He "declared racial prejudice criminal and a violation of the 'law of love' and . . . believed disobedience to slavery was obedience to God."[8] Wow! Replace the words *racial prejudice* with *racism*, and we might be on to something for the twenty-first century.

JOSIAH HENSON

Some say Josiah Henson was the model for the famous slavery-era novel *Uncle Tom's Cabin*. Whether or not that is true, he was still quite a character. His biography states that after slaving away for years, a plan was hatched for him to buy his freedom. But the unscrupulous enslaver tricked him out of the money he had saved to buy his release. Later, rather than honoring his promise to sell *him* to *himself*, the enslaver sent Josiah to New Orleans to be sold. The person assigned to transport him was also the enslaver's nephew.

On the way to the slave auction, the nephew becomes sick. Henson's sense of responsibility kicks in, and he nurses the young man back to health. For his trouble, the enslaver raises the price for Josiah. He figures Josiah's

---

6. History.com, "Underground Railroad," para. 9.
7. Urrrborderland.omeka.net, "White Abolitionists," para. 2.
8. Urrrborderland.omeka.net, "White Abolitionists," para. 3.

bent toward loyalty will increase his value. His change of heart towards Josiah did not happen because he was the person who saved his nephew's life. It was done for a less than noble reason. He believed that his property now came with verifiable proof of trustworthiness. That is amazing, isn't it?

Now let us read Henson's own words about his trip to be sold. "I am to be taken by my master and owner . . . to a place and condition where my life will be shortened and more wretched. Why should I not prevent this wrong if I can by shortening theirs?"[9] My sense of American-style justice and fair play says he would have been totally justified in freeing himself by any means necessary. What do you think?

Earlier in his biography, he described what his life was like. According to Henson, "Our lodging was in log huts, with no other floor than the trodden earth, in which ten or a dozen persons . . . might sleep."[10] He then describes the meager meals and the lack of clothing to protect them from the elements. He laments the selling of family members that he will never see again. In Henson's mind, "The natural tendency of slavery is to turn the master into a tyrant, and the slave into a cringing . . . victim of tyranny."[11] What follows are his memories of his chance for revenge.

> My eyes fell on Mr. Amos who was nearest to me; my hand slid along the axe handle. I raised it to strike the fatal blow,—when suddenly a thought came to me, "What commit a murder and you're a Christian?" I had not called it murder before. It was self-defense,—it was preventing others from murdering me,—it was justifiable, it was even praiseworthy. But now, all at once, the truth burst upon me that it was a crime. I was going to kill a young man who had done nothing to injure me, but obey the commands he could not resist.[12]

What a heart! But this shows we miscast the cruel reality of slavery, don't we? We rarely refer to it as evil. I watched *Schindler's List* again, and the similarities in the treatment of Jewish people and Africans were hard to miss. Yet our children are taught that one was a horror, while the other was just an unfortunate part of history. We can excuse some awful behavior by just renaming it. Jesus says, "Love your neighbor as yourself,"[13] adding there is no greater commandment. Maybe the enslavers should have defined neighbor differently. Maybe we should too!

9. Henson, *Life of Josiah Henson*, 53.

10. Henson, *Life of Josiah Henson*, 12.

11. Henson, *Life of Josiah Henson*, 10.

12. Henson, *Life of Josiah Henson*, 55.

13. Mark 12:31, NIV.

Henson and his family eventually made their way to Canada. Once there, he rescued hundreds of enslaved people. He founded a community that was one of the final stops on the Underground Railroad. One interesting fact is that they received help from some Native Americans during their journey. These people engaged in Tikkun Olam while risking their status, which was only marginally "higher" than the escaping Africans.

Isn't it interesting that the Native people lived out a Scripture many Christians ignore? "When a foreigner resides among you in your land, do not mistreat them. The foreigner residing among you must be treated as your native-born. Love them as yourself."[14] Christians dismiss many of the statutes found in the book of Leviticus because they are in the "Old Testament," meaning useless to some. It might be time for Christians to rethink whether or not the Hebrew Scriptures matter. They certainly mattered to Jesus.

Returning to the apple tree metaphor used earlier, we can see that Judaism is not only our tree but also our roots. Remember, Christianity would not exist without Judaism. Rabbi Aharon Lichtenstein writes, "Relation to the primary source is felt not only with respect to the text [Hebrew Scripture] or its content. It is felt, in a personal vein."[15] For example, I am a Black African, but I was born in the US. In that sense, I am an African American. Similarly, I am a Christian and a minister. Since I was born of the Hebrew Scripture, I am as much a part of them as I am a part of America. Let us talk more about the Hebrew Scriptures.

TORAH: THE BOOK OF LIFE

Paul M. van Buren wrote a series of books titled *A Theology of Jewish-Christian Reality*. I want to close this part of the chapter with a few of his insights about why Judaism should matter to today's Christian. Van Buren calls our attention to the fact that the Christian Bible begins with Israel's Torah. What is Torah? It is part of the Hebrew Scriptures and more than a book to religious Jews. Rabbi Sacks indicates, "Torah is God's book of humanity and each of us is a chapter in an unfinished story. Its words form our covenant with heaven."[16] And this is one practical benefit of Torah that goes unnoticed. When a first-century rabbi named Joshua ben Gamla made it possible for all Jewish children to study Torah, our model of publicly funded education was born.

---

14. Lev 19:33–34, NIV.

15. Lichtenstein, *Leaves of Faith*, 11.

16. Sacks, *Genesis*, 11.

Van Buren suggests Christians do not realize how Jewish people have "continued to read, preserve, interpret, and live from those Scriptures."[17] He adds that this misunderstanding of Judaism can lead to discrimination against Jewish people. He tells us Christian deafness to Torah has led to a "misunderstanding of 'Law' and 'Gospel,' a polarity of the church's invention."[18] And I believe this polarity distorts and limits the Christian vision of God.

One misunderstanding discussed in evangelical churches is the nature of the 613 commandments found in Judaism. The 613 commandments (mitzvot) include "248 positive commandments [do's] and 365 negative commandments [do not's]."[19] I often portrayed observing these mitzvot as the means by which Jewish people believed they would gain heaven. Today I see them differently. Judaism is not only about individual salvation, it is also about collective blessing. Allow me to illustrate. I live in an incorporated suburb of Austin, Texas. My city has its own charter and civic codes distinguishing it from Austin.

In my area there are rules designating which way garage doors must face. They cannot face the city street. There are noise restrictions that differ from Austin's. And so on. Some could see them as unnecessary, even trite. But they are guidelines put in place to ensure I know what it means to be a good citizen of my community. Correspondingly, rabbi Eliezer Berkovits believes the commandments are "an expression of God's care for and confidence in"[20] us to live responsibly. Now let us continue drawing parallels between Jewish ethical codes and the civic codes that Americans obey every day.

For years I contrasted these mitzvot with the Christian doctrine of grace, to imply that Judaism was a religion of laws and Christianity was one of freedom. I preached that the 613 rules were onerous. I did that without ever complaining about the large number of pages in my city's civic codes. That makes me a hypocrite, right? Thankfully, I wouldn't characterize these mitzvot that way today. I understand that ethics and community are central aspects of the Torah. And as Rabbi Soloveitchik notes, Torah is concerned with "our thoughts, feelings, and commitments."[21]

Ramban [Nachaminides], an influential sage, points to Deuteronomy 6:18 as a summation of Jewish ethics. It reads, "Do what is right and good

17. Van Buren, *A Theology of Jewish-Christian Reality Pt. 2*, 26.

18. Van Buren, *A Theology of Jewish-Christian Reality Pt. 2*, 26.

19. Hecht, "613 Commandments," line 1.

20. Berkovits, *God, Man and History*, 110.

21. Soloveitchik, *Visions and Leadership*, xi.

in the Lord's sight, so that it may go well with you." The commandments, like civic codes, are in place to improve our lives. Rabbi Goldstein writes, "By living in tune with Torah, we live in tune with our soul; by living a true Torah life, we nurture and expand our spiritual selves."[22] I will use my friend Rudy one last time to illustrate Rabbi Goldstein's point about the practical nature of Torah. Rudy is a nonobservant or nonreligious Jew. And yet he follows the precepts of Torah and observes Judaism's holy days. His commitment to living Torah makes him one of the most ethical people I've met.

Judaism and the Jewish people have contributed much to the world. It is shameful the price they've had to pay along the way. The fact that they have continually faced persecution exposes one fallacy of the human experience. You can't be a "good person" when you treat others unjustly. Moses listened to God in Egypt, and the Jewish people were freed from slavery as a result. Throughout this book, I have used examples of African chattel slavery to remind us that the self-described most democratic society in human history did the following: They appropriated land that was already occupied. Then they enslaved millions of Africans after taking them thousands of miles from their homes. This was done by people who claimed to follow the moral precepts of the Bible. It is not acceptable to ignore that history and minimize its horrors. That is because we cannot avoid the aftereffects.

Mount Sinai is where Moses received Torah. He listened, and what was heard freed an entire people group. Rabbi Sacks writes, "With the revelation at Sinai, something unprecedented entered the human horizon, though it would take centuries, millennia, before its full implications were understood. At Sinai, the politics of freedom was born."[23] That demonstrates that God is a God of freedom and justice. But human insecurity produces political models where the powerful exclude the poor and less powerful and look down on them. Insensitivities like these epitomize injustice. Sadly, this seems to be an age-old practice.

The histories of Greece and Rome suggest that democracies self-destruct when freedom is not granted to all. That is additional proof of the divine origin of Torah, and it is a good thing Moses listened. A popular adage in my tradition encouraged people to "do what Jesus did." Perhaps adding, "hear what Moses heard" would be good too. Then we might make justice and peace a priority like he did. In the next chapter, we will see that Jesus "welcomed" in order to instruct a different people group how to live the Torah.

22. Goldstein, "Word of Torah," para. 11.

23. Sacks, "Mount Sinai and the Birth of Freedom," para. 18.

CHAPTER 9, PART ONE

Christianity

JESUS WELCOMED

IF SOMEBODY TELLS YOU they are a Christian, what do they mean? Allow me to rephrase that. If someone tells you they are a Christian, what do you hear? To better understand what a Christian is, it might be good to know what a Christian was. Geographically speaking, "Christianity began in Jerusalem as a Jewish movement fulfilling Jewish hopes, promises and expectations."[1] Then it swept through Alexandria and other parts of the Mediterranean. Simultaneously, it circulated around Africa before arriving in Rome.

Theologian Thomas Oden reminds us that, "Judaism and Christianity have their roots in the story of a people formed in the interface between Africa, and Asia. Jews and Christians would travel from Egypt to Jerusalem"[2]— and presumably from Jerusalem to Egypt. For example, the Coptic Church of Egypt dates its founding to 42 AD. Hence, there is more to the Christian story than starting in Rome to be splintered by Martin Luther.

Best-selling author Tom Holland wrote a fantastic book named *Dominion*. On the cover is an image of the crucified Christ with tawny brown hair. The book's premise is that Jesus on the cross sparked the most important political event in Western history. Holland himself puts that in stronger terms, writing, Christianity "is the single most transformative development

---

1. Tennent, *Theology of World Christianity*, 3.
2. Oden, *How Africa Shaped the Christian Mind*, 16.

in Western history."[3] He believes Christian assumptions permeate every facet of Western society, whether religious or not.

It is true that our faith is the foundation of Western culture. However, Jesus was Jewish, and Christianity has included Europeans and others from its inception. And guess who else we find at Christianity's birth? Africans. During the first three or four centuries, Africans were among the most influential church leaders. Their names were Tertullian, Augustine, Cyprian, Athanasius, and Origen. It is critical for you to understand that, present-day biases aside, Christianity's formation happened in Europe, Asia, *and* Africa. Thus, these three locations gave rise to a variety of spiritualities.

Have you ever wondered why white church culture discourages dancing? Winton-Henry notes that "at the beginning of nearly every culture dance arose at the foundation of collective spiritual life."[4] She then asks the question about whether or not Jesus danced. If we asked most Western Christians if Jesus danced, they would probably answer, "That is silly." Comically speaking, they could argue Jesus might have tripped over his white robe while dancing. Dance is unacceptable to some whose piety centers on sermons and singing. But if you can sing and clap in church, why not dance? Author John Fisher argues that "the Spirit of God dances."[5] In fact, "He dances right under the noses of those who don't believe in dancing."[6] What is this about? The idea is similar to the Theyyam dance mentioned earlier.

Our Orthodox and Roman Catholic brothers and sisters accept that material objects can be sacred. But most Protestant versions of Christianity frown on such beliefs. In contrast, African people see drums as sacred objects. That gets to the heart of the matter. Finn writes, "The drum plays a significant role in every facet of Africans' lives: birth, initiation . . . war, death and in the religious life of the community."[7] Drumming leads to dancing, and dance is a vital part of African spirituality. That is frowned on by many Christians, even though the Bible says the body, mind, and spirit are parts of our spiritual makeup. It is not humanly possible to separate the three. Yet many versions of Western Christianity only permit church attenders to use one, the mind. Here is why.

Western Christianity's position on dance stems from its views about those pesky Africans. According to Ehrenreich, the Greek culture that spawned Western Christianity had "a danced religion much like the

3. Holland, *Dominion*, 13.

4. Winton-Henry, *Dance—the Sacred Art*, 2.

5. Fischer, *Real Christians Don't Dance*, 123.

6. Fischer, *Real Christians Don't Dance*, 123.

7. Finn, *Bluesman*, 83.

savages."[8] Over time Western antipathy for everything "savage" affected how we do church. Said another way, it affects what we don't do in church. As stated, Africans drummed and danced their way through life. That included their religious practices, and therein lies the rub. During the slavery era, drums were viewed by enslavers to be instruments for plotting their demise. So they prohibited drumming among the enslaved people. Where they lacked the power to do that, they attached a social stigma to drumming and dancing.

The quieting of the drum brought an end to dance in the Western church, including many African American churches. Donald Matthews notes that as far back as the 1700s, it was "required that any respectable [white] Christian—or Westerner for that matter—look upon the heathen [including Jewish] religious practices with disdain."[9] To underscore this point, Ehrenreich writes of a time when a white "Presbyterian missionary found a black Jamaican in what they called *Myal* dance"[10] and characterized him as crazy.

The Myal dance "is associated with a type of religious observance . . . The dance shows a wide range of body movements, extensive use of space and violence of action. These are done by throwing the body on the ground and by acrobatic feats."[11] How the minister interpreted what he saw leads us to the most common reason why dancing in white churches doesn't happen much. And that is, "We don't, because they did!" Racial division is largely the result of similar thinking only applied to a wide range of issues.

WHY BOTHER?

Does faith have any value? A similar question appears on page 250 of the book titled *Faith vs. Fact*. I have a strong anti-binary bent, so the title convinced me to buy the book. I just had to read what an author who saw the world in extremely rigid either/or binaries had to say. True to form, his book is a polemic against all faiths. However, he did reserve his harshest criticism for the Abrahamic faiths under discussion here. He sees faith as incompatible with science in the same way many believe Black and white people are socially incompatible, meaning they are best kept separate. I would add that many Westerners hold one or both of those views to one degree or another.

8. Ehrenreich, *Dancing in the Streets*, 12.

9. Matthews, *Honoring the Ancestors*, 49.

10. Ehrenreich, *Dancing in the Streets*, 119.

11. Jis.gov.jm, "Myal," para. 11.

What was just said is not opinion or conjecture. Churches would not be losing membership, and the news headlines would not contain so many examples of racial conflict, if it were not the case. Unfortunately, we process many of them as isolated incidents, recast the facts, and move on. Coyne engages in a similar recasting of facts when he concludes that faith does not have much value. He believes the world would get along just fine without it. Coyne may see all of Christianity negatively due to the self-focused variety that is popular in many circles. Who knows? That type of disenchantment with faith is happening with a lot of people in Western society. Below are some postulations Coyne believes are indisputable about faith.

> What would we lose in a world without faith would not be the good things—the art and literature, the fellow feeling that inspires us to help others, the moral impulses [as we'll see Europe is largely nontheistic, but hardly a hotbed of immorality] . . . On the secular side, we wouldn't have homeopathy or other non-religious forms of "alternative medicine," and there would be less opposition to global warming and vaccination. Debates about abortion, universal health care, and much of politics would be far more informed by facts, though, of course, they'd still involve subjective preferences.[12]

I love that he admits his fact-based society might sometimes give way to subjective preferences. Isn't that what humans throughout history have always done? Facts are fine until they no longer serve a purpose. Then they are replaced with new ones, even if they contradict the old. Coyne then speculates what else we would lose if religion disappeared. He writes, "We'd lose the harmful tenets of beliefs that rest on the certainty of God-given morality: the dysfunctional aspects of society that in the absence of religion would find little support."[13] In the block quote above, Coyne parenthetically extols the virtues of secular European morality. He implies that politics free of faith would result in a more just society.

Please consider this. Was religion ever cited as the cause of the carnage of the last century? If not religion, then what was the seedbed of those atrocities? Politics! With that in mind, think about these numbers: "An estimated 40,000,000 to 50,000,000 people died during World War II. Among the Allied powers, the U.S.S.R. suffered the greatest total number of dead: perhaps 18,000,000. An estimated 5,800,000 Poles died . . . about 298,000 Americans died. Among the Axis powers, there were about 4,200,000 German deaths

---

12. Coyne, *Faith vs. Fact*, 250.
13. Coyne, *Faith vs. Fact*, 251.

and about 1,972,000 Japanese deaths."[14] Do the math yourself. Subtract the American and Japanese death totals from even the low estimate, and what do we have? We come away with over 25,000,000 Eastern and Western European fatalities.

Remember a quote from an earlier chapter that said one group was able to absolve themselves from race matters? Here, we have a similar idea occurring. The people group Coyne holds up as being capable of developing morality separate from religion were the ones responsible for that violence. However, they avoid taking responsibility for it. But as Josef Joffe points out, "For about 2000 years, Europeans excelled at massacring one another."[15] Yet history's atrocities are often masked by a perfume called justification. We also employ it to conceal many current bad acts. Unfortunately, we spray it on the odors emanating from racism as well.

FAITH: OUR MORAL LIVES DEPEND ON IT

People who reject faith believe human beings have an innate good and evil monitor. They think people do not need anything external to themselves to make moral decisions. However, a problem surfaces when others watch the moral choices made by these folks. Their inconsistent behavior patterns suggest their moral monitors must not be plugged in. People like Sam Wells and Richard Dawkins, who believe we can be moral if left alone, are in deep denial about human history. Rather than thinking of evil as an inborn tendency, they tend to write it off as a series of mistakes resulting from secondary causes.

People are not always good and there is no running away from that. Judaism speaks of each person being born with the spark of God. In the Iona Community, we recognize that as God's image-bearers, we have something in us "planted more deeply than all that is wrong." Those concepts speak to different types of innate goodness. But each one requires a choice to become actuated. Facts about morality are not subjective unless one wants or needs them to be. That is why religion will always be necessary for a just society. You cannot have a just political system without a moral underpinning. And human history has shown this to be an immutable fact.

I was part of the hippie movement that hoped love could triumph over evil. John Lennon sang, "All you need is love," to usher in world peace. We thought, yeah, man, that is true. The Bible says, "Whoever claims to love

14. Britannica.com, "How Many People Died in World War II," para. 1.
15. Joffe, "Where Have All the Warriors Gone?," line 2.

God yet hates a brother or sister is a liar."[16] That passage seems to suggest loving others is the mark of Christianity, yet, as Rabbi Sacks has pointed out, "there is no general rule to tell us when love is the right reaction."[17] A moral code helps to define love, otherwise we are left with subjective speculations about what love is. Loving God's way is never subjective, it is objective, and there is a purpose.

THE HEART OF CHRISTIANITY

The gospel is called "good news," and it should produce the courage to live ethical lives. Since Jesus died for the entire world's sin, the good news must include everyone. The calling of Abraham's progeny didn't end with Judaism. Christians should participate in activities like Tikkun Olam too. The problem is some want a faith free of responsibility. Racial backgrounds influence the attitudes of America's Christian youth about ethics. In one study, an African American teen said, "If you are gonna dedicate your life to something. If you are gonna believe in something. If you are gonna worship something. It is not about you."[18] The white teens in the study had a different understanding. For them, "God is there to serve their needs whether forgiving them or making them feel better."[19] In terms of the beliefs of many Christians, that contrast might apply across the board.

But Jesus' life was a prophetic call for all to follow. Jesus put it this way: "Greater love has no one than this: to lay down one's life for one's friends."[20] Yet many who purport to follow in his steps refuse to even lay down their politics, favored social standing, or religious opinions for someone else's good. My friend Paul Louis Metzger suggests we engage others "heart to heart and life to life."[21] That is faith as it should be.

Unfortunately, like our two-party political system, we have liberal and conservative churches, and they couldn't be more different. In general, liberal churches see Christianity as part of everyday life. Their faith is a matter of reflection and action. As we say in our community, "In work and worship, God is with us." What does that look like? Social theorist James Davison

---

16. 1 John 4:20, NIV.

17. Sacks, *Essays on Ethics*, 45.

18. Christerson et al., *Growing up in America*, 122.

19. Christerson et al., *Growing up in America*, 124.

20. John 15:13, NIV.

21. Metzger, *Connecting Christ*, xxi.

Hunter offers us one example, writing, "We are to be fully present to each other in the community of faith and fully present with those that are not."[22]

Generally speaking, conservative churches are not like that. Separate compartments are used for living out faith. There is a high priority placed on participation in organized church activities such as attendance, small groups, short-term mission trips, etc. In this case a person's daily witness is de-emphasized. Michael Kogan highlights another difference: "Conservative churches love victors and liberals victims."[23] Let me break that down. Jesus' victory over sin would be celebrated by one side, while the other would find solace in God's rescue effort during the exodus. It is common for some to ignore the other side's emphasis, or question their legitimacy. But God cares about life's winners and losers equally. That is the good news.

We won't solve those religious paradoxes here, but hopefully my story will provide material to help you find answers that work for you. My faith journey began as a mainline Baptist kid. Then I became an ordained evangelical pastor, followed by serving as a Pentecostal missionary. After returning to the US, I became involved in the Emergent Church movement. Then I was received into the Anglican communion before landing in the Iona Community, formed within the Church of Scotland. My local faith community is called Bridging Austin, whose purpose it is to bridge the "unbridgeable." The significance of that will become clear shortly. For now, please remember my observations are not criticisms.

22. Hunter, *To Change the World*, 244.
23. Kogan, *Opening the Covenant*, 227.

CHAPTER 9, PART TWO

My Journey

I GREW UP IN the American Baptist Church, a mainline denomination. It exists because the Baptists had a split over slavery. The Southern Baptists were on the proslavery side of that split. They were a very large evangelical body and fought hard to keep slavery legal. Scripture was used to support their position by twisting passages to imply God favored the practice. Author Robert Jones writes, "No segment of White Christian America has been more complicit in the nation's fraught racial history than white evangelical Protestantism."[1] It may be wise to file that.

On the flip side, Jones notes that white mainline Protestants "have remained to this day a consistent voice for racial equality among white Christians."[2] The push to recognize the humanity in all was true of my family's church. They took the commandment to "love others" seriously. My church wasn't white. And we were not evangelical. But we sure were faithful to biblical Christianity. Interestingly, my parents said I should love members of a white denomination that saw me as a devil—the Mormons.

When I was growing up, the official position of the LDS Church was that God blackened our skin to mark a curse God had placed on us. They did manage to say it respectfully and positively, though. For example, the "Church of Jesus Christ of Latter-day Saints taught that their membership, 'shall be a white and a delightsome people' . . . The LDS Church also restricted black members' participation in important rituals and prohibited

1. Jones, *End of White Christian America*, 167.
2. Jones, *End of White Christian America*, 178.

black men from becoming priests."[3] However, that exposed a major flaw. That is because the only way one could reach the highest heavens was to be a priest.

The church's second president was named Brigham Young. When addressing his ban on Black males to the priesthood, Young's great-granddaughter has claimed he wasn't a racist. She somehow managed to say "believers may never fully grasp why the ban was needed at all, only that . . . 'it was God's will.'"[4] Unfortunately, today, just like then, exclusionary racial policies can be easily reframed as non-racist. They can also be framed as God's will. Thankfully, my family taught me to "love those who hate you." Without that, I couldn't survive in our Western culture. And loving, not excluding, really is God's will.

THE EVANGELICAL YEARS

Now let's look at my time as an evangelical pastor in a seeker church. There is a song by The Who titled "The Seeker." The term "seeker" was also the basis for one style of church that was popular in the 1990s. The song's theme was that a seeker wouldn't get what they wanted until they died. The seeker church's message implied the opposite. A person could get what they wanted by attending church. Churches exist to enhance lives. For example, during this period I asked a young friend what he wanted in a church. The answer was donut holes and plenty of video games. My friend may have been eight or nine years old at the time. But asking someone what they want in a church is central to the seeker church model.

One pastor here in Austin got right to the point by calling the attenders "customers." In a sense, he's right, since this model works on the same principles as other types of businesses. Being relevant to the culture, one of the stated goals soon gave way to rubber-stamping it. The pastors believed leadership should do all it could to not offend potential attenders. If parts of the Bible offended the culture, they were not presented or were reinterpreted. All of the planning had customer satisfaction in mind. Once, I totally agreed with that philosophy, believing a bigger church would follow. Of course I convinced myself I was pursuing excellence for God. But I became disillusioned when I found myself taking attender satisfaction surveys similar to political polls every year. Here is how that started.

Before surveys became fashionable, I had to learn what was important to the congregation by waiting for people to voice expectations following the

3. Green, "When Mormons Aspired to Be a 'White and Delightsome' People," para. 3.

4. Stack, "Brigham Young may have started," para. 12.

weekly service. One woman at the church I served in Sherman Oaks, California, illustrates this perfectly. Following one service she said, "I like this church because it has kick-a** worship, a positive message, and donuts." As with any market-driven enterprise you have competition for market share. A musician named Tommy Walker became the song leader at a church called Christian Assembly and had a hit album on the worship charts. With that success came a better band. Guess what? It wasn't long before she began attending that church. Thankfully, it was a part of my denomination, and that soothed the sting. However, I vowed never to lead a church to compete with another, like many of my peers.

Later I worked at another seeker-style church, only not as the lead pastor. As you know, I performed music at some very large venues and before hundreds of thousands of people. Shows of this type require meticulous planning. That means you spend a great deal of time arranging lights and making sure the sound system is as good as it can be. You take time to decide where people stand on stage so that everyone looks their best. Then there are volume concerns, so the players don't overpower the audience. The show received most of the energy and not the music.

As it happened, I found the same operating procedures in that seeker church. Staff meetings focused on how the service would be received. On Tuesdays, we discussed how last Sunday's service went and what could have been done better. It was a total deja vu experience for me. That was because, in one setting, the show took precedence over the music. In the other setting, the service presentation took precedence over spirituality. Prayers were rarely said, and spiritual matters were seldom discussed during staff meetings. It was like attending a board meeting at a corporation. We were a business and functioned like one. What's wrong with that? Nothing. I am not sharing this to be critical. And I am not saying there is something wrong with doing church like this. I am only sharing another stop on my journey.

PENTECOSTAL BLIND SPOTS

Julaine and I were Pentecostal missionaries to Belize, Central America. During this time, I had a friend who took over the pastor position at a church in my denomination. The neighborhood was transitioning from being white to Black. He discovered minutes of a leadership meeting from several years before. What had been discussed was the "problem" of the new arrivals, Black people. They did not discuss what could be done to stop them from attending. But they did discuss ways to ensure Black people would not want to come. They decided against changing the style of worship, music, etc., effectively saying, "Please don't come." Much of the racial tension that occurs is not the result of what Black people do; it is about where they are.

Author Yossi Halevi, writing about Jewish/Muslim tensions, suggests that estranged cultures often see the other's daily activities as a threat. Hence, minority advancement in "their society" is viewed negatively. And they even see their presence as dangerous. For example, as long as Black people remained in their place physically, economically, and socially, things were fine. But today, when Black people question the justness of that arrangement, many white Christians become defensive. There may be no clearer example than how the word *woke* is perceived in white evangelical circles. I was in a Bible study with several white friends with whom I have been close for years. One night this comment was passed: "I hate people who are into wokeness." I let the comment go unchallenged because I was unfamiliar with the term at the time.

Later I Googled the word and found this definition: "alert to injustice and discrimination in society, especially racism."[5] Then I asked myself, "Why would anyone who loves Jesus hate that?" I did find that some had repurposed the term so it meant Black racism against white people. They bemoaned reverse racism while forgetting who originated the concept of racial categories. That is why injecting terms like "reverse racism" into the conversation is a red herring, meaning "something intended to be misleading or distracting."[6] Besides, shouldn't the church be about pursuing inclusion, equality, justice, and compassion?

Perhaps it is Black people's rejection of having their lives negatively affected by racial categories that is bothersome to them. Whatever the reason, we should not lose sight of this. Black people have never passed laws to enslave white people's bodies, restrict their movement, or prevent their constitutional rights from being accessed. In the book *Pathologies of Power*, Paul Farmer suggests constitutional rights are not operational if social and economic rights are not extended to all. He writes, "There is heated opposition to the enlargement of the rights concept."[7] The expansions of Black rights have been the bone of contention in conversations on race since the founding of the nation.

Historically, it has been white people that have decided who is entitled to which right and when. Believing that reverse racism exists would be rational if Black people were able to treat white people similarly. But it simply

5. Lexico.com, "Woke."

6. Lexico.com, "Red herring."

7. Farmer, *Pathologies of Power*, 9.

cannot be accurate until Black people have that kind of power. This is why the notion that reversing this type of racism only shows a lack of understanding of the term. Apart from that, I would argue that it is white racial dispassion that needs to be reversed more than imagined Black racism.

THE EMERGING CONVERSATION

When I returned to the US from Central America, I saw something special happening in a youth movement called the Emerging Church. The air was filled with hope and possibilities. In all honesty, I believed we were on the verge of igniting a spiritual revolution. I hoped its impact would exceed the Reformation's—and surpass the influence that the Jesus People movement had on American culture. I was present at the birth of the hippie movement, which shaped a nation's youth culture to the point that the rest of the world was caught up in its vortex. But that is what Christianity is all about, hope and possibilities, isn't it? It is not quantifiable, it is a qualitative thing, and so keeping it real is what matters. According to Graham Ward, "Faith announces a vision of ethical life, of a good that is, can, or should be lived out."[8] That is simply what faith does.

It is too early to be accurate about why the Emergent movement ran out of gas and dissipated. Our movement was not a denomination but a group of like-minded people seeking to move Christianity beyond the borders imposed on it by denominations and political slants. In other words, it was keeping the spiritual, spiritual, while holding all else loosely. During this period, I read theological and philosophical insights from a cross section of thinkers, such as Jacques Derrida, Richard Rorty, Martin Heidegger, Stanley Grenz, Robert Webber, and N. T. Wright. People young and old and from all walks of faith or no faith were welcomed. That is a journey I am still on, which leads us to where I am today.

BRIDGING AUSTIN

Julaine and I lived in Belize City for a little over eight years. One strange thing happened during our time there. After five or six years we became culturally Belizean. We knew we still had a house full of furniture in storage in Los Angeles. But that life was very far removed from us. Belize was still a British protectorate when we moved there, having gained independence a

---

8. Ward, *How the Light Gets In*, ix.

decade earlier. In fact, our home was a reconfigured British Army barracks, hence the nickname "the Barracks."

I was in for quite a surprise at a mall in my former hometown in the US when my Belizean roots took center stage. A woman who waited on me asked where I was from. The reason she was curious was because she liked my accent. At the time I was offended. I felt like telling her Manhattan Beach but gave in and said Belize. Why the change in my speech? It was due to the BBC and a few US movie channels being the only television available at the time. We became binge viewers of British mysteries, leading us to appreciate everything British. Over time, and little by little, we became more British than American in many respects. It was weird and still is, but that is where we are.

While in Belize, I moved past the right to focus on what was left politically. I am saying that being away that long caused me to lose interest in American politics, right or left. The truth is I never gained it back. I no longer see life politically as a result. Many of my friends and family find that difficult to understand. Many times, I sense they don't believe it is possible. The news is filtered through a political strainer, and I stopped watching it around 2003. Since then, I haven't watched a newscast unless I am in an airport or at the gym.

Recently a friend was exasperated about an upcoming election. When I told him I was unaware it was happening, I could see disbelief written all over his face. But it was true. The upside of this is I am able to interpret life spiritually not politically. Even if politics and religion intersect at times, I view them as separate. Because as Halevi notes, "The laws of faith, after all, act differently than the laws of politics."[9] Politicians pursue power, but Christians are to pursue peace. By understanding this, political tensions no longer affect my spiritual well-being. And I am able to appreciate the religious beliefs of people who disagree with each other politically.

As a reminder, racial tensions are the source of what concerns me most. That is because I know Jesus welcomed us to welcome others. Sadly, I see many Christians who refuse to make a move in that direction. My work history includes small churches and large churches. I have worked in Black churches and many that were 90 to 95 percent white. Yet, I have only known of one truly multiethnic church. I know of several white churches with a good number of Black attenders, but that are still stylistically white. That is because their worship style is like other white churches, only darker-skinned people attend. What happens is this: If Black people are willing to attend on those terms they are welcome. But minority preferences are

9. Halevi, *Entrance to the Garden*, xvi.

disregarded in these scenarios. We try to do multiethnic church differently. The unfortunate thing is few people get it. This will explain why.

EVERYONE SHOULD HAVE A STAKE IN IT

What follows is a parable I use at Bridging Austin that was recently published in *The Coracle*, the magazine of the Iona Community. Imagine that you are the largest cattle rancher in the state of Texas. Your daughter has been in California for the past two years, attending the University of California, Berkeley. If you are unfamiliar with Berkeley's location, it is about ten miles east of San Francisco. And true to the region's recent past, it is a bastion of progressive activism. If you know anything about Texas, then you know Texas is the polar opposite in terms of political leanings.

The holidays are approaching, and you decide you want your daughter to come home for Christmas. As an added incentive, you tell her you will send the family jet to fly her and any friends she'd like to invite to the ranch. You are not aware that during her time away, she has embraced a vegan diet, and every one of the friends she is bringing is a vegan too. You slaughter your most prime beef to prepare the best meal possible. Your guests arrive, but no one eats. You are perplexed and offended. Why are they abstaining after you have given them the best of everything? Jesus might have answered you this way, "You did well to invite them, but since you did not consider their preferences first, you did little to welcome them."

Bridging Austin is a welcoming community because, as Hunter writes, "To welcome the stranger . . . is to welcome Christ. Believers or non-believers, attractive or unattractive, admirable, or disreputable, upstanding or vile—the stranger is marked by the image of God."[10] Consider these words from Jesus, "I pray that all of them may be one." That is the objective of this chapter. That is what Jesus walked this earth to do—engage in a radical welcome that makes outsiders feel more like insiders.

My life and ministry are guided by the sacred texts of Judaism and Christianity. According to Sangor Goodhart, a process has been established for accessing that guidance. And that is "to let oneself be addressed by the voice that speaks through it [the texts] and respond with one's life."[11] Does that voice say your happiness is God's primary concern? Or does it say God is more concerned with how you treat others? The latter is the one I hear. As Christians, we are to have concern for the well-being of everyone. That includes those we are in conflict with. That is hard to do. Personally, I have

10. Hunter, *To Change the World*, 245.

11. Goodhart, *Prophetic Law*, 135.

learned to love people I know disapprove of me. It is possible for you too. However, it requires a different way of thinking to execute. Next we look at Islam. The Muslim faith calls on its adherents to follow a similar path but in response to a different text.

CHAPTER 10, PART ONE

Islam

MUHAMMAD CALLED

AT ONE TIME, MARTIN Luther King embodied the African American civil rights movement. Today, most Christians are too young to know he was not that popular among many white people. Some even claimed his activities were detrimental to his race. I remember people calling him Martin Luther "Coon" and laughing about it. That hurt, but it would typically be followed by, "It is just a joke." There was relief, even joy, in many circles when he was shot. Initially, I didn't realize how much hearing hatred of that type affected me. Emotionally, it was the equivalent of reading "crucify him" about Jesus. Muslims likely hear similarly hurtful "innocent comments" on a daily basis. My experience occurred in northern California, one of the most progressive regions in the US. I can only imagine the response to King's shooting in other parts of the country.

I did not have to speculate when another civil rights leader named Malcolm X was shot. Many people were ecstatic and showed it. Who was he? Why would people feel free to openly cheer the death of another human being? He was a leader of the Black Muslims, that is why. Most white people in the country either feared them or hated them. At that time, the word *Muslim* was enough to strike fear in most Americans, and it still does. Pop quiz. What goes through your mind when you see a Muslim woman with a hijab (scarf) on her head? Depending on the answer, it may be easier for you to grasp the following. When the word *Black* was placed in front of Muslim, it gave many a license to empty both barrels of contempt at them. Muslims, who are these people who practice strange customs and who often come from strange lands? Let us turn to the History website for a brief overview.

> The word "Islam" means "submission to the will of God." Followers of Islam are called Muslims. Muslims are monotheistic and worship one, all-knowing God, who in Arabic is known as Allah. Followers of Islam aim to live a life of complete submission to Allah. They believe that nothing can happen without Allah's permission, but humans have free will. Islam teaches that Allah's word was revealed to the prophet Muhammad through the angel Gabriel. Muslims believe several prophets were sent to teach Allah's law. They respect some of the same prophets as Jews and Christians.[1]

As stated in the last chapter, I view faith through spiritual lenses, not political ones. I said that because many people tend to conflate politics and religion. That can result in confusing political rhetoric with the Christian gospel message of love and grace. Correspondingly, my interest in the Palestinian/Israeli situation lies in the conflict between observant Jews and religious Muslims over matters of faith, not the land. From the outside, they may appear similar, but they are quite different. Political debate between Palestinians and Israelis over land has only produced, to borrow from Barbera Bowe, "conflict at the boundaries and internal conflict about what and where those boundaries should be."[2] But religious and cultural disagreements run much deeper.

Israeli journalist Sheri Oz says this about Jewish-Muslim relations in Palestine: "In Israel, Jews often call Arabs 'cousin' and that is because, as Arabs, they are our cousins. They are not our cousins by virtue of them being Muslims. We do not call Malaysians or Pakistanis cousin because, while they are Muslims, they are not Arabs."[3] Rabbi Sacks has a different view. He writes, "Jews and Muslims both trace their descent from Abraham—Jews through Isaac, Muslims through Ishmael. The fact that both sons stood together at their father's funeral tells us that they too were reunited."[4] For this chapter and this book, cousins or brothers, "human oneness isn't a philosophical notion or a moral imperative but simply a fact."[5]

But when people are faced with cross-cultural conflict, it is common to deny that we are all humans of equal substance and value. Those who wish

1. History.com, "Islam," lines 14–27.

2. Knowles et al., eds., *Contexting Texts*, 97.

3. Oz, "Rabbi Sacks," para. 2.

4. Sacks, "On Judaism and Islam," para. 12.

5. Halevi, *Entrance to the Garden*, xvii.

to undermine the acceptance of our oneness do it in any way they can. Here is the problem. Many of our social problems intensify when we reject the biblical view of human oneness. This process has been facilitated by the use of language. For example, one historian suggests American race relations were "complex and controversial" from 1834 until 1891.

Complex? Hardly. Moreover, isn't that the same vocabulary people use to avoid ameliorating tensions between Jews, Christians, and Muslims? Friends, peacemaking isn't complex. Just think, Black/white relations suffer because one side tells themselves they are essentially superior. But a belief in one people group's superiority over another did not evolve out of complexity but choice. Loving the other is not a complex concept. But it requires humbly making different choices. Besides, faith means having the courage to face complex issues with hope.

Judaism, Christianity, and Islam claim Abraham as their father. Could God have purposely created these religious siblings to test their willingness to love each other? Scary thought. Mark Gopin writes, "World religions have a reservoir of prosocial values.[6]" Love is the one prosocial value central to all three religions. In light of today's political climate, that statement would be hard for many to believe. Sadly, I would imagine the majority of Western Christians do not view Islam positively. That needs to change.

It would be wise to learn about a religion before condemning the people who practice it. We have more in common than you think. For starters, Judaism, Christianity, and Islam are book religions. That means Scripture is at the center of all three. Additionally, they each have a version of the "Golden Rule." There is more. Each aspires to improve society, even if they differ on how that should be accomplished.

An Israeli author who regularly engages Christians and Muslims writes, "Islam contains those qualities necessary for peacemaking—humility before God and an acute awareness of morality."[7] He also believes a day is coming when the three faiths can live together as one. This comes from someone living in the midst of the Palestinian-Israeli conflict. What is holding us back from even considering the possibility? Fear of the unknown? Maybe we all should learn about the religion of others. We would most likely strengthen our own beliefs in the process. My parents taught me a philosophy that has served me well. Look for the good in others before you focus on the differences.

6. Gopin, *Between Eden and Armageddon*, 10.
7. Halevi, *Entrance to the Garden*, xvii.

ALLAH: GOD

If you were asked this question, "Does God exist?," what would you say? If the follow-up question was "What does God do?," how would you answer? It may surprise you to learn that according to Pew Research, "nine in ten Americans believe in a higher power, but only a slim majority believe in God as described in the Bible."[8] The survey addresses our second question by recording that "nearly all adults who say they believe in the God of the Bible say they think God loves all people regardless of their faults."[9] Wow! What a different world we would live in if people really believed that! However, those are not the questions I want to challenge you with. This is: Is there a God of the Bible, and a different God in the Qur'an? If yes, how different?

That question and more is covered in an excellent book by Miroslav Volf. The title of the book is simply *Allah*. As we proceed, I want to ask a favor. Let us assume, even if it is just for the purpose of discussion, that Allah and the God of our Bible are the same person. Volf summarizes the important elements of that position this way: "Muslims and Christians have a common God and partly overlapping understandings of God and God's commands."[10]

As a reminder, the headings of this section's three chapters read, Moses listened, Jesus welcomed, and Muhammad called. My experience has been that Muslims absolutely believe that part of their calling is to love their neighbors. And Volf assures us that "Muslims have a sufficiently robust moral framework to pursue the common good."[11] For those who see the world politically, that might seem hard to fathom. But as stated in the last chapter, things change when you look at the world through spiritual lenses. Besides, there are only two basic ways human beings interact. They either cooperate with other people, or they enter into conflict with them.

For the remainder of this chapter, I will focus on the overlaps Volf mentions. Keep in mind that this book is about contrasts and not comparisons. I am not looking to compare the differences between the three Abrahamic faiths so that we can argue about them. On the contrary, I am contrasting the differences to better understand and appreciate them. My reason for this is that "there is an infinite set of possibilities associated with

8. Pewresearch.org, "When Americans Say They Believe in God," line 1.

9. Pewresearch.org, "When Americans Say They Believe in God," para. 14.

10. Volf, *Allah*, 187.

11. Volf, *Allah*, 14.

religious institutions . . . in terms of peace and violence."[12] I will focus on pursuing the former while acknowledging the latter happens. Now allow me to share real-life examples of some Muslims engaging in Tikkun Olam or, to restate Volf, pursuing the common good. The stories focus on two loving human beings. The fact that they are Muslim is an added bonus.

MOMO

In the Judaism chapter, I said there were not many people I loved more than my friend Rudy Greene. The same can be said of another friend named Momo. As opposed to being Jewish, Momo is a devout Muslim who practices the Sunni version of Islam. Submitting one's will to God can be an immediate concern for some. Here is why. Placing religion and obedience in the same sentence is a problem for many Christians. We can find the phrase "must do something" very troublesome. Moreover, many believe that strict adherence to religion is the source of much of human conflict. Especially the kind practiced by "radical Islam."

But one way to translate the word *Islam* is obedience. And according to Adam Walker, "Obedience is a fundamental part of Islam which sits at the very heart of the system . . . In practice, [it] greatly facilitates both spiritual and temporal advancement."[13] Consequently, obedience is a calling from God. And obedience differs from an obligation in this way. An obligation is a requirement or a duty, whereas obedience is voluntarily submitting one's will to another. Though it can be challenging, a calling from God is one of obligation in addition to one of obedience. Let me share what I observed Momo do in response to his call.

Momo is a property owner with a master's degree from a small village outside Dhaka, Bangladesh. He came to the US on a temporary visa and folded into the thriving Bangladeshi community in South Florida. As soon as he and his spouse, Naima, arrived, they began working minimum wage jobs and applied for work visas. Julaine and I frequented the 7-Eleven where Momo and his wife worked multiple shifts. Momo and Naima have worked the same jobs for the twenty years we have known them. They have worked tirelessly to provide the means for their son to succeed. Momo and Naima are devout and strict adherents to every tenet of the Muslim faith.

Momo fasts during Ramadan, even when working double eight-hour shifts on his feet. We've been present when he looked so weak we wondered how he could stand. My admiration grew when I saw how dedicated he was

12. Gopin, *Between Eden and Armageddon*, 11.
13. Walker, "Obedience," line 5.

to God, knowing that people at the church where I worked would find such discipline off-putting. His unwavering obedience paid off because his son is due to start his medical residency soon. When we saw Momo last year, he told us it will be a family honor when Starz becomes a doctor. He says that it could not have happened without God. As we left the store, he looked at us, flashed a half-smile, and said, "I'm happy."

A mutual friend from his hometown in Bangladesh came to the US and started a business. As the business grew, he became more Westernized and began drinking. That led to multiple sexual liaisons. Momo and I have had numerous conversations about Western morality. Since he knew very little about my faith, Momo asked if this kind of behavior was acceptable in Christianity. I told him no. He asked, why then, if most people in the US are Christian, does this happen so much? Perhaps the answer is that we just take it for granted that we should be able to pursue happiness without being constrained by religion.

Volf offers this observation from Philip Rieff's *Triumph of the Therapeutic*: "Contemporary culture is a culture of the managed pursuit of pleasure, not a culture of the sustained endeavor to lead the good life as defined by sacred narratives."[14] In most of the churches I have served, when Abraham's name comes up, faithfulness and blessing are not far behind. But we find a different take on Abraham's importance if we eavesdrop on a conversation between an Israeli Jew and a Palestinian Muslim.

Halevi writes, "Abraham's task as a monotheist . . . was to shatter the idols of fragmented consciousness and restore humanity's 'spiritual sight,' our ability to perceive oneness."[15] This reveals that people of faith can read the same text and reach entirely different conclusions, doesn't it? It took me years to realize that different and wrong are not synonyms. Now I will share a story about a time a Shia poured out his love.

HOUSE OF SAID

In the late 1970s, I lived in Sherman Oaks, California. I went to New York for an extended period to perform with many of the *Saturday Night Live* musicians. I used to play pool at a small bar named The Back Door. In a moment of excitement, I told people there I would be away from the city for a while. I left my home unattended, and it wasn't long before I received a call telling me I had been burgled. This was not a situation where a burglar popped a window and rifled through drawers taking valuables. Apparently,

14. Volf, *Allah*, 215.

15. Halevi, *Entrance to the Garden*, 38.

one of my "friends" from the bar pulled a truck up to my house and proceeded to remove everything of value from it. That included guitars and other musical equipment, furniture, and appliances. They did a complete sweep. Needless to say, I returned home demoralized.

I decided to leave the Los Angeles area and return to Santa Cruz, where I rented a small apartment. An adage attributed to novelist Thomas Wolfe says a person can never return home. I found that to be true. The music scene had changed dramatically during the nine years I had been gone, and it was difficult to fit in. I bounced around several situations before joining a band with a guitarist from a Shia Muslim family. I soon began thinking that I needed to return to my real home in Los Angeles, but I was not yet emotionally healed from the burglary. He sensed my frustration and procured a copy of the Qur'an for me in case my instability was spiritual.

Next, he did something above and beyond. He offered to let me stay in a rental property for free, giving me time to regroup. After a while, I moved back to Hollywood before eventually landing back in Manhattan Beach. This man from a Shia Muslim background actually lived these words of Jesus, "I was a stranger and you invited me in," to the letter. This proves there are similar principles in Islam as well. Consider this Sunnah, literally habitual practice, from Islam, "Be kind to your neighbor and you will be a believer."[16] Momo and the house of Said turned me into a believer that, despite my Western bias, Islam is a religion of love and peace. In answer to our question about who these people are, they are people just like you and me!

16. Ahmed, "Golden Rule in Islam," para. 5.

CHAPTER 10, PART TWO

Following Mohammad

An Obligation of Obedience

LIFE IS ABOUT CHOICES, and determining which are best is at the heart of religion. For our Jewish brothers and sisters, choices are based on the prescriptions found in the Torah given to Moses. For the Christian, it is the person of Jesus. And for Muslims, it is Muhammad's calling. Let us take a moment to review Islam's basic tenets: "God sent our Prophet Muhammad to us, in order to call us to salvation and bliss . . . He told us in it about the [religious] obligations that would enable us to attain"[1] that salvation and bliss. The concept of obligation is integral to Islam and Judaism. In Islam, one of those obligations is "abiding by the orders of Allah and avoiding His prohibitions."[2] For the "grace-only" type Christian, any mention of religious obligation is considered pointless. If that is you, let me challenge you a little.

The book of James implies obedience builds character. Antinomianism is the view that grace frees the Christian from any obligation to obey the law. But is Islam's call to obedience any different from these words that Jesus spoke, "Anyone who loves me will obey my teaching"?[3] And remember, much of the Jesus story itself revolves around his submission and obedience to God's will. That indicates *obey* is not a dirty word. The truth is, Christians have the same duty to obey as our religious siblings. The fact that Muslims place a high value on submitting their will to God is a good thing. Islam's call to obedience isn't answered by uneducated backward people stuck in

1. Khaldun, *Muqaddimah*, 354.
2. Yahya, "Obedience to Allah."
3. John 14:23, NIV.

the fifteenth century. As you can see from my experiences, Islam is a beautiful religion that produces equally beautiful people.

COMMONALITIES

Beautiful people? The thought may cross your mind, "I would never say anything like that about Muslims!" Earlier I alluded to the prosocial values Gopin found in Islam. But I knew when I included the quote that many would find the statement counterintuitive. To many Westerners, Islam means 9/11 suicide pilots and suicidal Muslims blowing themselves up as an act of hatred and defiance against our way of life. But given a chance, Islam can be perceived very differently. Imagine if, instead of feeling superior to Muslims, we viewed them as people doing their best to make their way through life, just like us. Would that allow for a change of perception of them?

As already mentioned, I was a missionary to Belize in the 1990s. An overseas missionary's job is to spread the good news of Jesus Christ worldwide. In 1493, Pope Alexander VI had the same understanding of Christian mission that sent me to Central America. That led him to believe Christian kings should send armies to bring people everywhere under the rule of the Roman Church. The pope issued a bull titled *Inter Caetera*, giving Spain and Portugal exclusive rights to colonize the Americas. It also mandated that they Christianize any savages found on the newly discovered lands. Today people argue about the pope's intentions because history suggests the bull was also used to justify the enslavement of Africans.

Whether the bull was a document misused by unscrupulous politicians, or overused by zealous Christian leaders, misses the point. Let us acknowledge that religious zeal and political greed contributed to a lot of suffering and death. My reason for pointing this out is twofold. One, these events were the genesis of the Western world's belief that it had a responsibility to take control of the earth's landmasses, inhabited or uninhabited. And second, what followed was an assumed right to categorize and classify everything within its control. Our lives are still affected by the aftermath of those decisions, culminating with the "it all started here" from an earlier chapter.

Now let us look at the attitudes of a different faith community, Islam, right around that time. Khaldun, the Muslim historian from the Middle Ages, writes, "In the Muslim Community, the holy war is a religious duty, because of the universalism of the Muslim mission and [the obligation to] convert everybody to Islam either by persuasion or by force."[4] Once again, a well-intentioned but misguided understanding of religious obligation leads a different group of people to engage in similar behavior. Maybe the only difference between Christianizing by force and getting people to submit to Allah by force is the time and place each event occurred. But as Rabbi Sacks points out, "Religion is at its best when it relies on strength of argument and example. It is at its worst when it seeks to impose truth by force."[5]

The pope's decree and Khaldun's history were written within one hundred years of each other. Imagine how different our world would be had the leaders of Islam and Christianity been amenable to sitting down and discussing their commonalities. Had each side renounced their "right" to engage in forced conversion to advance their religion, millions of lives would have been spared. We should never wage war to physically, economically, or socially convert people to our faith. If politicians want to declare wars to impose their will, that is on them. As religious people, we are to be advocates of peace, and anything short of that is a failure on our part.

SIMILARITIES

Google Raymond Bernal Jr., and you will find a park in San Jose, California that bears his name. He was the bass player in my teenage band and a close friend. He has been honored in this way because while serving in the Army, he placed his body on a live hand grenade to save his platoon. Why did he do it? He perceived his sacrifice was for the good of America, a.k.a. the common good. Apart from the sadness that resulted from my friend losing his life, there was an irony in his act of heroism. He made the ultimate sacrifice at a time when many of his friends were actively protesting the war in Vietnam.

Was he the same type of crazy we label those we call terrorists? Or was his willingness to lay down his life for his beliefs different because we agree with the cause? What we have here are two drastically different interpretations of the same action. The political leaders in San Jose viewed Ray as a hero. But at the time, many of his contemporaries viewed him as a fool who wasted his life for nothing. The truth of the matter is this: Bernal may have viewed his responsibility as similar to a Muslim adage that says, "Great aims, to be achieved, call for great sacrifices, and success in making a reality out of them comes at high cost."[6]

4. Khaldun, *Muqaddimah*, 183.

5. Sacks, *Not in God's Name*, 234.

6. Razwy, "Sacrifices of Muhammad For Islam," line 1.

To be clear, I am not suggesting moral equivalence here. But I am saying this: It is possible to find similarities if we take our eyes off the justification for an act. This illustrates the problem with judging someone based on your perception of their motives. Please read the following few sentences slowly and carefully. According to author Jerry Coyne, Damon Linker "sees human altruism as a gift from not just God, but the Christian God, who performed his own act of self-sacrifice by sending Jesus to an earthly death."[7] As spot on as that quote is, it does not include Jesus' willingness to give up his life in the same manner as Bernal and an Islamic fundamentalist.

Wait a minute, that is not right! What moral comparison are you trying to make between a war hero, the Son of God, and a terrorist? None. I do not believe that altruistic evil exists. I am merely pointing out that their sacrifices were similar, even if the reasons for them differed. The belief in something bigger than oneself is foundational to religious faith. Sayyid Ali Asghar Razwy says Muhammad "sacrificed all his personal comforts, and all his material possessions for the sake of Islam."[8] Moses sacrificed his private life, and Jesus his public life, for the well-being of others. See a pattern here?

I will conclude this chapter with a reminder that the perceived divide between Jewish sects, Islamic sects, and Christian denominations is not as significant as you might imagine. We now know that Muslims are not that dissimilar from us. One article I read indicated the three faiths have much in common. For example, they each believe it is important to do good works and extend hospitality. In their own ways, each seeks justice and pursues peace. In addition, all three hold that faith is centered around loving God with all one's heart and mind.

Now for the takeaway. For starters, the Jewish community is covenantal and we need more than one covenantal community. Secondly, Christian churches provide a welcoming environment, and they set a good example for all to follow. The Muslim community understands obedience as an imperative. And faith-filled living is something we should all strive to do more of.

In summary, it would be a God-honoring endeavor to have each distinct faith community live out the positive elements of the other. Let us embrace the possibility God uses all three faiths to facilitate national, racial, and religious border crossings. I want to be as clear as possible about the borders separating faith communities. Crossing these borders would not eliminate or dilute any distinctions. In contrast, the elements that make each religion unique could be acknowledged and appreciated. A scenario

7. Coyne, *Faith vs. Fact*, 168.

8. Razwy, "Sacrifices of Muhammad For Islam," para. 9.

like this would result in each community being affirmed by the other. We could then view the other faiths as family members contributing to the good of the whole. Remember, there are billions of people worshiping Israel's God today because of these three Abrahamic faith traditions.

Epilogue

Dancing Across National, Racial, and Religious Borders

GREG GRAFFIN, LIKE ME, is an author and musician. He wrote a book titled *Population Wars*. Graffin is also the lead singer in a band named Bad Religion. However, the comparisons end there because this book was written to encourage you to participate in "good religion." It is there that humanity has the best chance of replacing social conflict with social peace. When writing about living things, Graffin writes, "All are members of populations. In the past these groups were easy to tell apart."[1] So far so good. Then he says we "considered some of them evil, some friendly, some wild and untamed, and some put here to serve our own selfish needs."[2]

The self-serving inclination in us that Graffin references is why we spent so much time discussing African chattel slavery, which epitomized that mindset. The fact that African slavery happened and continued for as long as it did matters. In its minutes from 1885, a Western Christian mission board acknowledged what many people would rather forget or deny, "Colored people in our country were taken by the hand of violence."[3] This has resulted in the creation of a race of homeless people erroneously called "African Americans." In truth, they are neither African or American. They are sojourners of African descent. Today, Black people live in places their ancestors did not choose. Moreover, even if they were granted the freedom to leave, they would need a passport to enter other nations. That is an overlooked consequence of American slavery.

Contrary to some beliefs, religion is not the source of conflict in the world. As we have just discussed, there is a desire in some to amass enough

1. Graffin, *Population Wars*, 1.
2. Graffin, *Population Wars*, 1.
3. Cloutier, *Bridging the Gap*, 147.

political power to control people, places, and things. That is the root of social conflict. And remember, in most Western countries, the state has prescriptive authority that religion lacks. Simply put, religion can't force the citizens of a Western country to do anything, whereas the state's coercive power is limitless. The premise of this book is that rather than politics, "religion emerges as a set of ideas that keep dance alive."[4] That dance is a dance of love and not power.

POWER

For a nation-state to exist, participation in its precepts must be mandatory. One example happened when the great South African peace activist bishop Desmond Tutu was slated to participate in a ceremony in Scotland for the Iona Community. He had to withdraw because his government seized his passport and would not allow him to leave the country. *The New York Times* reported, "The action made good on a threat twice issued by Prime Minister P. W. Botha to retaliate against the Bishop."[5] This is not just a legal matter. It is also a sociological problem. A person of Dutch descent controlled the body of an African person on African soil.

But if birthplace determines nationality, why did a Black African need a pass and permission from a person of European descent to travel? Because Tutu lived where even the white people needed a license from the state to "carry [transport] . . . black people."[6] Yes, white people needed permission to give Black people rides on their own soil. Think through all that says. Bishop Tutu couldn't leave one nation-state, and what follows is an example of Black people's difficulty getting into others.

Harvard professor Charles Mair, who is white, recalls a time traveling in Europe, when "as an American waving a blue passport I pass through the Schengen [EU] barriers easily . . . for people of color the border scrutiny is far more intense."[7] The issue here is about more than an interaction with a state agency. It is crucial to understand this one overlooked fact about people of African descent. Our place in the world is not a consequence of evolution or environmental pressure but the misuse of power. The result is ethnic-cultural nationalism and racism. Regrettably, a society built on an ethnic-cultural foundation will always require there to be some kind of "other" to survive.

---

4. Lamothe, *Why We Dance*, 93.

5. Special to *The New York Times*, "South Africa Seizes Tutu's Passport," para. 4.

6. Paton, *Cry, the Beloved Country*, 81.

7. Maier, *Among Empires*, 86.

OTHERNESS

Dance can be the object and also the agent of social control. Marches performed during parades and rites of passage are two examples. There is a purpose in these types of dances. One example is a Fourth of July parade in the US. Chad Seales writes, "In towns with a historical African American presence, southern whites used parades to contest public spaces."[8] White participants would march through Black areas behind a float carrying the parade's beauty queen. The beauty queen was always white, regardless of how many Black people lived in the area. This sends a message to Black folk that this is the personification of beauty. And as Seales notes, "To say otherwise was unnatural and outside the bounds of what they considered a divinely sanctioned social order."[9] When people are devalued this way, self-loathing can follow similar to the kind Malla Nunn expressed earlier.

REVISITING CULTURE AND IDENTITY

Much of our social conflict stems from the moving targets of culture and identity. Is identity neutral? Kwame Appiah says, "Many people have the idea that the normative content of an identity should be determined essentially by its bearer."[10] That says, "You decide." The shift from having the state or biology frame one's identity to personal choice will be challenging for many. For example, I know of an eleven-year-old child who no longer wanted to be a boy and decided to identify as a girl. He asked his parents for permission, and his request was met with an emphatic no!

Not to be deterred, the kid went to school and told the officials of his desire. The school affirmed his decision and allowed him to change his name on the school rolls. That ignited a fierce confrontation between the parents and the school board. How it was resolved is not the point. The point is that in our age, identity is fluid. I will leave it to you to decide the right or wrong of it. My goal is to prepare you for it.

YES, I'M READY: TO BORDER DANCE

Border dancing has some basic rudiments, such as flexibility, stretching, and strength. In order to "dance the dance," here are a few essential

8. Seales, *Secular Spectacle*, 61.
9. Seales, *Secular Spectacle*, 59.
10. Appiah, *Ethics of Identity*, 67.

requirements: Have the ability to accept challenges, be flexible enough to be changed by them, and be strong enough to live out those values even through difficulty. The decision to change directions is often "dripping" with difficulty. In matters of white and Black race relations, it can come from both sides. To overcome that requires effort, intention, and perseverance. With that in mind, let us revisit our three themes.

Nationalism

At times, working through conflict requires building relationships with people from an unpopular geography. For example, hanging out with people from places labeled a terrorism hotbed. I remember a rash of books after 9/11 containing variations on the title "Why do they hate us?" They were written to Western readers without ever considering that the people whose cities experienced surgical air strikes killing their loved ones were asking the same question. We must be honest with ourselves about the following truth: most nations came into existence through the use of force. And violence has been the tool of choice to maintain them.

Race

I saw a video on Facebook the other day. In the clip, a very large Black man was in an airport lounge waiting for a flight. While waiting, he struck up a relationship with a young white kid playing video games. The man appeared to be in his forties, while the kid looked about ten years old. Comments on the clip mostly focused on the fact that the kid was blond and the man was Black. The funniest aspect, or the possibly saddest, is one white person tried to show how accepting and tolerant he is by writing, "I didn't even notice he was black until I read the other comments." Really? The guy was huge! The goal of this book is not to have you "miss the color" of another person but learn to appreciate it.

Religion

Recently, my older brother reminded me that our American Baptist family ate fish on Friday. Most of the kids in our neighborhood were Roman Catholic immigrants from Mexico. At that time they didn't eat meat on Fridays but fish was allowed. My mom believed that our family should be in solidarity with them as Christians, even though they were different kinds of Christians. That is when I learned to embrace rather than reject the religious other.

Today I am in solidarity with people of other faiths while maintaining a firm commitment to my tradition. These relationships are not established by debating religious beliefs but by respecting the intrinsic humanity of the other. Religion's main function is to bring people together. That is why Christians especially, are to treat *everyone* with dignity. No excuses!

DANCE STEPS TO LOVE

1. Expand your conception of normal. That means don't just conceptualize a new normal, live it into existence. I scoured the internet hoping to find various concepts of beauty from around the world. I did that because I included the white beauty queen as an example of a group in power imposing their preferences on others. Hopefully, you do not think I am against white women being presented as beautiful. Quite the opposite, my wife is white and beautiful. But so are millions of other women wherever they are located, and whether or not they are white.

    Diversity fills the universe, but many people fail to see all of its beauty. That is due to their cultural blindness. One article titled, "Going Global," by Kate Kasbee, featured examples of female beauty from the US, Brazil, India, France, and Korea.[11] Due to her preference for lighter skin, the author overlooked the beauty of women living on a continent with over a billion people. To be clear, lighter-skinned beauty is not the issue—the issue is the denial of darker-skinned beauty. But there *is* beauty in all of God's design, even among the most discounted and excluded.

2. Empathize with the historical past of the other *and* their experiences. That means placing yourself in the position of the person you are engaged with. Don't treat what is being said by them as a news report to be analyzed. My white friends often doubt me when I describe treatment I receive that's similar to the extra scrutiny from government agents that Maier observed. If you recall, he commented on watching darker-skinned people receiving treatment that was different from his as a white professor in the public sphere. My friends dismiss most of those types of examples by comparing them to how they were treated in similar circumstances. That exposes the missing component in race relations, empathy.

    When discussing race, try starting from the other's point of view and then approach the specific subject matter. I know that can sound

11. Kasbee, "Going Global."

akin to being on deck when the *Titanic* is sinking, and the ship's captain asks you to jump in the water to save someone. Put simply, it may sound like an exercise in futility. The parallel is this. As you metaphorically stand in your safe spot on the deck, you can at least listen empathetically to the panicked screams of those crying out in fear. Then you can get a real sense of what they are experiencing. Just think, in this illustration, you know you will soon join them. We all know that being on top, the deck in this instance, doesn't last forever. You never know, that might apply to all of life, including racial hierarchies.

3. Encourage those outside your present social network and racial group. I believe people who struggle with food insecurity or financial instability are probably not lazy. They simply do not have the social capital the average middle-class American has. That alone limits their options. If you perceive someone as not living up to community standards, my advice is, do not complain about them, become an encourager. That will help make somebody's tomorrow different.

LOVE WAITS ACROSS THE BORDERLINE

The borders we have approached in this book were human creations. Many of these borders were formed by guns, ships, and cannons. Others were developed via racialized science. Still others were advocated for by rigid religious dogmas. The common denominator is that they exist because we accede to their legitimacy. One example is the borders of a nation-state are respected until they are overrun. That we readily accept the new borders established by the victor proves that the old ones only existed in our minds. The borders that separate people are different. They are created by human failure and exist in our hearts. It is my sincere hope that something you have read will inspire you to dance the dance of love. During this dance, meaningful and lasting social relationships can be established across national, racial, and religious borderlines. Please remember:

"While I dance I cannot judge, I cannot hate,
I cannot separate myself from life. I can only be joyful and whole.
That is why I dance."[12]

—HANS BOS

12. Finestquotes.com, "Hans Bos."

Bibliography

Abarim-publications.com. "Horos." https://www.abarim-publications.com/DictionaryG /o/o-r-o-sfin.html.

Ackroyd, Peter. *Foundations*. New York: Thomas Dunne, 2011.

Adekoya, Remi. "Biracial Britain: why mixed-race people must be able to decide their own identity." https://theconversation.com/biracial-britain-why-mixed-race-people -must-be-able-to-decide-their-own-identity-154771.

Ahmed, Ismail. "The Golden Rule In Islam." https://www.siasat.com/golden-rule-in-islam-2025296/.

Akala. *Natives: Race & Class in the Ruins of Empire*. London: Two Roads, 2019.

Alexander, Kathy. "Gangsters, Mobsters & Outlaws of the 20th Century." https://www. legendsofamerica.com/20th-gangsters/.

Amazon.com. "William Dalrymple, *Nine Lives: In Search of the Sacred in Modern India*." https://smile.amazon.com/gp/product/B0036S4D38/ref=dbs_a_def_rwt_ hsch_vapi_tkin_p1_i6.

Anderson, Benedict. *Imagined Communities*. London: Verso, 1991.

Appiah, Kwame Anthony. *The Ethics of Identity*. Princeton: Princeton University Press, 2007.

Azquotes.com. "Ameen Rihani." https://www.azquotes.com/quote/967173.

———. "Samuel Johnson." https://www.azquotes.com/quote/769693.

———. "W. E. B. Du Bois." https://www.azquotes.com/quote/936768.

Bachman, Eric. "4 Steps Toward Demolishing the 'Concrete Ceiling' that Black Employees Face." https://www.forbes.com/sites/ericbachman/2020/06/11/4-steps -toward-demolishing-the-concrete-ceiling-that-black-employees-face/?sh=69c 50f96c7f0.

Les Ballets nègres scrapbook, Sc MG 526, Schomburg Center for Research in Black Culture, Manuscripts, Archives and Rare Books Division, The New York Public Library. https://nyplorg-data-archives-production.s3.amazonaws.com/uploads/ collection/generated_finding_aids/scm20962.pdf.

Bantum, Brian. *Redeeming Mulatto*. Waco, TX: Baylor University Press, 2010.

Baptist, Edward E. *The Half Has Never Been Told*. New York: Basic, 2016.

Begbie, Jeremy S. *Theology, Music, and Time*. Cambridge: Cambridge University Press, 2000.

Berkovits, Eliezer. *God, Man and History*. Jerusalem: Shalom, 2014.

Blaisdell, Bob. *Great Speeches of the 20th Century*. Mineola, NY: Dover, 2011.

Bolland, O. Nigel. "Belize." https://www.britannica.com/place/Belize.

Boys, Mary C. *Has God Only One Blessing?* New York: Stimulus, 2000.

Brainyquote.com. "Cecil Rhodes." https://www.brainyquote.com/authors/cecil-rhodes-quotes.

———. "Clint Smith." https://www.brainyquote.com/quotes/clint_smith_893500.

———. "Zazie Beetz." https://www.brainyquote.com/quotes/zazie_beetz_909034.

Brewer, John D. *Ethnography*. New York: Open University Press, 2000.

Britannica.com. "Christine Jorgenson." https://www.britannica.com/biography/Christine-Jorgensen.

———. "Circumstantial Evidence." https://www.britannica.com/topic/circumstantial-evidence.

———. "Fire." https://www.britannica.com/dictionary/fire.

———. "How Many People Died in World War II." https://www.britannica.com/question/How-many-people-died-during-World-War-II.

———. "Zeus." https://www.britannica.com/topic/Zeus.

The Britannica Editors. "Chivalry" https://www.britannica.com/topic/chivalry.

Brock, Sebastian. *The Luminous Eye*. Kalamazoo, MI: Cistercian, 1992.

Burt, Ramsey. "Elroy Josephs." https://www.taylorfrancis.com/chapters/edit/10.4324/9781315306551-16/elroy-josephs-hidden-history-black-british-dance-ramsay-burt?context=ubx.

———. "Elroy Josephs and the Hidden Costs of British Black Dance." https://dora.dmu.ac.uk/bitstream/handle/2086/18949/Burt_Elroy%20Josephs_final.pdf?sequence=2.

Cahill, Thomas. *The Gift Of The Jews*. New York: Anchor/Nan A. Talese, 1999.

Cannadine, David. *The Rise and Fall of Class in Britain*. New York: Columbia University Press, 1999.

Chabadgreenwich.org. "Heaven and Earth." https://www.chabadgreenwich.org/templates/blog/post.asp?aid=2197590&PostID=85095&p=1.

Chabad.org. "What is Machloket l'Shem Shamayim?" https://elmad.pardes.org/wp-content/uploads/2015/09/Machloket-lshem-shamayim-for-Lesson-Plan.pdf.

Christerson, Brad, et al. *Growing up in America*. Stanford, CA: Stanford University Press, 2010.

Clary, Mike. "Defense Pulls Pro Wrestling Into Murder Trial." https://www.latimes.com/archives/la-xpm-2001-jan-25-mn-16948-story.html.

Cloutier, Mary Carol. *Bridging the Gap: Breaching Barriers*. Eugene, OR: Pickwick, 2021.

Conrad, Jennifer. "70 years on, how China sees the Korean War." https://supchina.com/2020/10/14/70-years-on-how-china-sees-the-korean-war/.

Coyne, Jerry A. *Faith vs. Fact*. New York: Viking, 2015.

Craemer, Thomas. "There Was a Time Reparations Were Actually Paid Out." https://today.uconn.edu/2021/03/there-was-a-time-reparations-were-actually-paid-out-just-not-to-formerly-enslaved-people/.

Crouch, Stanley. *Kansas City Lightening*. New York: Harper Perennial, 2014.

Crown, Kayode. "FedEx Reinstates Pay For Black Driver Who Alleged White Men Chased, Shot At Him." https://www.mississippifreepress.org/20765/fedex-reinstates-pay-for-black-driver-who-alleged-white-men-chased-shot-at-him.

Dalrymple, William. *Nine Lives: In Search of the Sacred in Modern India*. New York: Knopf, 2009.

Dan, Joseph. *The Teachings of Hasidism*. Millburn, NJ: Behrman House, 1983.

Danceask.net. "Eskita Dance of Ethiopia." https://danceask.net/eskista-dance-ethiopia/.

———. "Top USA/American Origin Dance Forms." https://danceask.net/top-american-origin-dance-forms/.

Daynes, Sarah, and Orville Lee. *Desire for Race*. Cambridge: Cambridge University Press, 2008.

Definitions.net. "Horos." https://www.definitions.net/definition/horos.

Derbew, Sarah. "Blackness in Antiquity." https://aeon.co/essays/how-does-an-ancient-greek-cup-challenge-anti-black-racism.

Diamond, Jared. *Guns, Germs, and Steel*. New York: W. W. Norton, 1999.

Dictionary.Cambridge.org. "Atomistic." https://dictionary.cambridge.org/us/dictionary/english/atomistic.

Dictionary.com. "Divide and Conquer." https://www.dictionary.com/browse/divide-and-conquer.

Dils, Ann, and Ann Cooper Albright. *Moving History/Dancing Cultures: A Dance History Reader*. Middletown, CT: Wesleyan University Press, 2001.

Dotros, Ron. "Freedom Jazz Dance." https://keyboardimprov.com/the-jazz-pianists-ultimate-guide-to-the-real-book-table-of-contents/freedom-jazz-dance-from-the-jazz-pianists-ultimate-guide-to-the-real-book/.

Doumbia, Adama, and Naomi Doumbia. *The Way of The Elders*. Saint Paul, MN: Llewellyn, 2004.

Eagleton, Terry. *Evil*. New Haven: Yale University Press, 2011.

Ehrenreich, Barbara. *Dancing in the Streets*. New York: Holt, 2006.

Elkins, Carrie. *Imperial Reckoning*. New York: Holt, 2005.

Emery, Lynn Fauley. *Black Dance*. Princeton: Dance Horizons, 1972.

Encyclopedia.com. "Dionysian Dance." https://www.encyclopedia.com/humanities/culture-magazines/dionysian-dance.

Etymonline.com. "Kin." https://www.etymonline.com/word/kin.

Fackenheim, Emil L. *To Mend the World*. Bloomington: Indiana University Press, 1982.

Faculty.fiu.edu. "Apollonian/Dionysian Dichotomy." https://faculty.fiu.edu/~harrisk/Notes/Aesthetics/Apollonian-%20Dionysian%20Dichotomy.htm.

Farberman, Brad. "Why Is Sun Ra Finally Having His Moment?" https://www.rollingstone.com/music/music-features/why-is-sun-ra-suddenly-having-his-moment-197156/.

Farmer, Paul. *Pathologies of Power*. Berkeley: University of California Press, 2004.

Finestquotes.com. "Hans Bos." http://www.finestquotes.com/author_quotes-author-Hans+Bos-page-0.htm.

Finn, Julio. *The Bluesman*. New York: Interlink, 1992.

Fischer, John. *Real Christians Don't Dance*. Minneapolis: Bethany House, 1988.

Foner, Eric. *Story of American Freedom*. New York: W. W. Norton, 1998.

Goldstein, Warren. "A Word of Torah." https://thejewishnews.com/2022/01/20/a-word-of-torah-why-the-giving-of-the-torah-is-a-turning-point-in-history/.

Goodhart, Sandor. *The Prophetic Law: Essays in Judaism, Girardianism*. East Lansing, MI: MSU Press, 2014.

Goodreads.com. "Leopold II." https://www.goodreads.com/quotes/10753944-i-do-not-want-to-miss-a-good-chance-of.

———. "Michael Jackson." https://www.goodreads.com/quotes/6536664-this-world-we-live-in-is-the-dance-of-the.

———. "Oscar Wilde—De Profundis." https://www.goodreads.com/quotes/317-most-people-are-other-people-their-thoughts-are-someone-else-s.

———. "Samuel Beckett" https://www.goodreads.com/quotes/123103-dance-first-think-later-it-s-the-natural-order.

Gopin, Marc. *Between Eden and Armageddon*. Oxford: Oxford University Press, 2000.

Gordon, Mike. "The Hired Gun." https://www.anchoragepress.com/news/the-hired-gun/article_ec.b03334-290b-5fcf-9f1e-238ea7459e42.html.

Graffin, Gregg. *Population Wars*. New York: Thomas Dunne, 2015.

Green, Alex. "Prof. Alex Green Interviews Rabbi Jonathan Sacks." https://arts-sciences.buffalo.edu/content/dam/arts-sciences/jewish-thought/documents/green-sacks-interview.pdf.

Green, Emma. "When Mormons Aspired to Be a 'White and Delightsome' People." https://www.theatlantic.com/politics/archive/2017/09/mormons-race-max-perry-mueller/539994/.

Green, Lauren. "Stereotypes: Negative Racial Stereotypes and Their Effect on Attitudes Toward African-Americans." https://www.ferris.edu/HTMLS/news/jimcrow/links/essays/vcu.htm.

Haenfler.sites.grinnell.edu. "Subcultures and Sociology." https://haenfler.sites.grinnell.edu/subcultures-and-scenes/the-deadhead-subculture/.

Haines, Jan Harper. "Idle Hour." https://www.alaskapublic.org/2014/11/06/the-idle-hour-country-club/.

Hanna, Judith Lynn. *To Dance Is Human*. Chicago: University of Chicago Press, 1979.

Halevi, Yossi Klein. *At the Entrance to the Garden of Eden*. New York: Harper Perennial, 2002

Hecht, Mendy. "The 613 Commandments." https://www.chabad.org/library/article_cdo/aid/756399/jewish/The-613-Commandments-Mitzvot.htm.

Hejazi, Walid. "Lessons in Chinese History." https://theconversation.com/lessons-in-chinese-history-as-america-shuts-off-from-the-world-99360.

Henson, Josiah. *The Life of Josiah Henson*. New York: Dover, 2015.

Hentoff, Nat. *The Nat Hentoff Reader*. New York: Da Capo, 2001.

Herder, J. G., and F. M. Barnard. *Introduction to Herder on Social and Political Culture*. Cambridge: Cambridge University Press, 1969.

Hill, Mike. *Whiteness: A Critical Reader*. New York: NYU Press, 1997.

Hirt-Manheimer, Aron. "Schindler's List: Separating Truth from Fiction." https://reformjudaism.org/schindlers-list-separating-truth-fiction.

History.com. "Islam." https://www.history.com/topics/religion/islam.

———. "Underground Railroad." https://www.history.com/topics/black-history/underground-railroad.

Hofstede-insights.com. "Country Comparisons." https://www.hofstede-insights.com/country-comparison/the-usa/.

Holland, Tom. *Dominion*. New York: Basic, 2019.

Hunt, Ellen. "It's not beige, it's not grey: it's greige—and it's why all our houses look the same." https://www.theguardian.com/lifeandstyle/2022/may/25/greige-color-paint-popular-interior-decorating-design.

Hunter, James Davison. *To Change the World*. Oxford: Oxford University Press, 2010.

Hutchinson, John, and Anthony D. Smith. *Nationalism*. Oxford: Oxford University Press, 1994.

Immigrationhistory.org. "Nationality Act of 1790." https://immigrationhistory.org/item/1790-nationality-act/.

Inspirationalstories.com. "Chinese Proverbs On Dancing." https://www.inspirationalstories.com/proverbs/t/chinese-on-dancing/.

Ivanhoe, Philip J., and Bryan W. Van Norden. *Readings in Classical Chinese Philosophy*. Cambridge: Hackett UK, 2011.

Jarry, Jonathon. "Are You There, Race? It's Me, DNA." https://www.mcgill.ca/oss/article/health-general-science/are-you-there-race-its-me-dna.

Jel.jewish-languages.org. "Tikkun Olam." https://jel.jewish-languages.org/words/576.

Jenkins, Richard. *Rethinking Ethnicity*. Thousand Oaks, CA: Sage, 1997.

Jis.gov.jm. "Myal." https://jis.gov.jm/information/jamaicas-heritage-dance-music/jamaicas-heritage-dance/.

Jluggage.com. "Countries Japan Colonized." https://www.jluggage.com/blog/history/countries-japan-colonized/.

Joffe, Josef. "Where Have All the Warriors Gone?" https://www.hoover.org/research/where-have-all-warriors-gone.

Jones, Aquil, and Joseph Tracy. "Black Workers at Risk for 'Last Hired, First Fired.'" https://www.dallasfed.org/research/swe/2020/swe2002/swe2002e.aspx.

Jones, Robert P. *The End of White Christian America*. New York: Simon & Schuster, 2016.

Kasbee, Kate. "Going Global: The Perception of Beauty Around the World." https://aedit.com/aedition/global-beauty-trends-the-perception-of-beauty-around-the-world.

Keralatourism.org."Theyyam Ritual Artform." https://www.keralatourism.org/artforms/theyyam-ritual/1.

Khaldun, Ibn. *The Muqaddimah*. Princeton: Princeton University Press, 2005.

Klasfeld, Adam. "Greg McMichael Never Used the Word 'Burglary' in Police Interview, Called Slain Ahmaud Arbery an 'A**hole': Officer." https://lawandcrime.com/live-trials/live-trials-current/ahmaud-arbery/greg-mcmichael-never-used-the-word-burglary-in-police-interview-called-slain-ahmaud-arbery-an-ahole-officer/.

Knowles, Melody D., Esther Menn, John Pawlikowski, and John J. Sandoval, eds. *Contexting Texts*. Minneapolis: Fortress, 2007.

Knowyourphrase.com. "Break the Ice." https://knowyourphrase.com/break-the-ice.

Knox, Robert. *The Races of Men*. London: Forgotten, 2018.

Kogan, Michael S. *Opening the Covenant*. Oxford: Oxford University Press, 2008.

Kreuger, Alyson. "What to Know About the Jewish Hora Dance." https://www.brides.com/hora-dance-5069553.

Lamothe, Kimerer L. *Why We Dance*. New York: University of Columbia Press, 2015.

Le Donne, Anthony, and Larry Behrendt. *Sacred Dissonance*. Peabody, MA: Hendrickson, 2017.

Lexico.com. "Altruism." https://www.lexico.com/en/definition/altruism.

———. "Choreography." https://www.lexico.com/en/definition/choreography.

———. "Cognitive dissonance." https://www.lexico.com/en/definition/cognitive_dissonance.

———. "Identity politics." https://www.lexico.com/en/definition/identity_politics.

———. "Red herring." https://www.lexico.com/en/definition/red_herring.

————. "Responsive." https://www.lexico.com/en/definition/responsive.

————. "Shaman." https://www.lexico.com/en/definition/shaman.

————. "Standing." https://www.lexico.com/en/definition/standing.

————. "Woke." https://www.lexico.com/en/definition/woke/.

Lichtenstein, Ahron. *Leaves of Faith*. Jersey City, NJ: KTAV, 2003.

Lindqvist, Sven. *Exterminate All the Brutes* London: Granta, 1997.

Loc.gov. "Africana Historic Postcard Collection." https://www.loc.gov/rr/amed/afs/africana-postcards.html.

————. "Tap Dance in America: A Short History." https://www.loc.gov/item/ihas.2002 17630/.

Maalouf, Amin. *The Crusades through Arab Eyes*. New York: Schocken, 1984.

Maier, Charles S. *Among Empires*. Cambridge: Harvard University Press, 2006.

Martin, Thomas R. *Ancient Greece*. New Haven: Yale University Press, 1996.

Mathabane, Mark. *Lessons of Ubuntu*. New York: Skyhorse, 2018.

Matthews, Donald H. *Honoring the Ancestors*. Oxford: Oxford University Press, 1998.

Mawusi, Kodzo. *African Theology*. Victoria, BC: Friesen, 2015.

Maxouris, Christina. "What we learned from testimony in the trial over Ahmaud Arbery's killing." https://www.cnn.com/2021/11/22/us/what-we-learned-ahmaud-arbery-trial-testimony/index.html.

Meredith, Martin. *The Fate Of Africa*. New York: Public Affairs, 2011.

Metzger, Paul Louis. *Connecting Christ*. Nashville: Nelson, 2012.

Miller, Peter M. *Principles of Addiction: Comprehensive Addictive Behaviors and Disorders, Volume 1*. San Diego: Academic, 2013.

Mishra, Pankaj. *Bland Fanatics: Liberals, Race, and Empire*. New York: Farrar, Strauss, and Giroux, 2020.

Mitchell, Arthur. "What Does Dance Give You?" https://quotefancy.com/quote/168 4678/Arthur-Mitchell-What-does-dance-give-you-The-freedom-to-be-who-you-are-and-do-what-you.

Morrisdances.com. "Bean Setting." http://www.morrisdances.com/cotswold/BeanSetting.html.

Naim, Asher. *Saving the Lost Tribe*. New York: Ballantine, 2003.

Najam, Adil. "The Conversation." https://theconversation.com/how-a-british-royals-monumental-errors-made-indias-partition-more-painful-81657.

Nationalarchives.gov.uk. "Indian Indentured Laborers." https://www.nationalarchives.gov.uk/help-with-your-research/research-guides/indian-indentured-labourers.

Nationalgangcenter.ojp.gov. "What is a gang?" https://nationalgangcenter.ojp.gov/about/faq#faq-1-what-is-a-gang.

Nesteruck, Alexi V. *Light from the East*. Minneapolis: Fortress, 2003.

Nh.gov. "Folk Life." https://www.nh.gov/folklife/learning-center/traditions/music-dance.htm.

Nmaahc.si.edu. "Handbill." https://nmaahc.si.edu/object/nmaahc_2013.144.

Noah, Trevor. *Born a Crime*. New York: One World, 2019.

Northrup, David. *Africa's Discovery of Europe*. Oxford: Oxford University Press.

Nunn, Malla. "I Grew Up Mixed-Race in Southern Africa." https://www.theguardian.com/books/2019/jul/05/i-grew-up-mixed-race-in-southern-africa-who-has-the-right-to-tell-my-story.

Oden, Thomas. *How Africa Shaped the Christian Mind*. Downers Grove, IL: InterVarsity, 2007.

Olusoga, David. *Black and British*. London: Pan, 2018.

Otto, Raphael. "On The Link Between African And Irish Music." https://wp.me/p11fCR-6o/.

Oz, Sherri. "Rabbi Sacks: Muslims are not our cousins," https://israelforever.org/interact/blog/rabbi_sacks_arabs_are_our_cousins_not_muslims/.

Pallardy, Richard. "Oskar Schindler." https://www.britannica.com/biography/Oskar-Schindler#ref1108462.

Paris, Peter J. *A Spirituality of African Peoples*. Minneapolis: Fortress, 1995.

Paton, Alan. *Cry, the Beloved Country*. New York: Scribner, 1987.

Pewresearch.org. "Jewish community and connectedness." https://www.pewresearch.org/religion/2021/05/11/jewish-community-and-connectedness/.

———. "Race, ethnicity, heritage and immigration among U.S. Jews." https://www.pewresearch.org/religion/2021/05/11/race-ethnicity-heritage-and-immigration-among-u-s-jews/.

———. "When Americans Say They Believe in God, What Do They Mean?" https://www.pewresearch.org/religion/2018/04/25/when-americans-say-they-believe-in-god-what-do-they-mean/.

Picturequotes.com. "Janice Tanton." http://www.picturequotes.com/i-care-about-the-human-race-and-i-strive-to-understand-it-quote-308656.

Pilgrim, David. "The Tragic Mulatto Myth." https://www.ferris.edu/HTMLS/news/jimcrow/mulatto/homepage.htm.

Razwy, Sayyid Ali Asghar. "The Sacrifices of Muhammad For Islam." https://www.al-islam.org/restatement-history-islam-and-muslims-sayyid-ali-asghar-razwy/sacrifices-muhammad-islam.

Rijksmuseum.nl. "Dionysus/Bacchus." https://www.rijksmuseum.nl/en/rijksstudio/subjects/dionysusbacchus.

Rose, Steve. "Julie Felix: the brilliant Black ballerina." https://www.theguardian.com/stage/2021/mar/04/julie-felix-the-brilliant-black-ballerina-who-was-forced-to-leave-britain.

Rosenzweig, Franz. *Star of Redemption*. Notre Dame: University of Notre Dame Press, 1985.

Ross, Janice. *Like A Bomb Going Off*. New Haven: Yale University Press, 2015.

Roy, Sanjoy. "How black dancers brought a new dynamism to British dance." https://www.theguardian.com/stage/2013/sep/20/black-dance-history-british-routes?CMP=gu_com.

Ryan, Jim. "Chubby Checker Looks Back." https://www.forbes.com/sites/jimryan1/2020/07/27/interview-chubby-checker-looks-back-as-the-twist-turns-6o/?sh=7158c23d7f28.

Sachs, Curt. *World History*. New York: W. W. Norton, 1963.

Sacks, Jonathan. *Essays on Jewish Ethics*. New Milford, CT: Maggid, 2016.

———. *Genesis: Book of Beginnings*. New Milford, CT: Maggid, 2009.

———. *The Home We Build Together*. London: Bloomsbury, 2003.

———. "Mount Sinai and the Birth of Freedom." https://www.rabbisacks.org/covenant-conversation/yitro/mount-sinai-and-the-birth-of-freedom/.

———. *Not in God's Name*. New York: Schocken, 2014.

———. "On Judaism and Islam." https://www.rabbisacks.org/covenant-conversation/chayei-sarah/on-judaism-and-islam/.

———. *To Heal a Fractured World*. New York: Schocken, 2007.

———. "The Way of Responsibility." https://www.rabbisacks.org/curriculum-resources/ten-paths-to-god/unit-10-responsibility/.

Saha, N., and J. S. Tay. "Origin of the Koreans." https://pubmed.ncbi.nlm.nih.gov/1510113/.

Saini, Angela. *Superior*. Boston: Beacon, 2019.

Sandset, Tony. *Color that Matters*. London: Routledge, 2014.

Seales, Chad E. *The Secular Spectacle*. Oxford: Oxford University Press, 2013.

Senate.gov. "DC Compensated Emancipation." https://www.senate.gov/artandhistory/history/common/civil_war/DCEmancipationAct_FeaturedDoc.htm.

Sibley, Natalee. "Whipping: A Physical Punishment of Slaves." https://transatlanticarchivespring2018.commons.gc.cuny.edu/2018/03/26/whipping-a-physical-punishment-of-slaves/.

Simon, Matt. "Fantastically Wrong: The Silly Theory That Almost Kept Darwin From Going on His Famous Voyage." https://www.wired.com/2015/01/fantastically-wrong-physiognomy/.

Solomon, Richard H., and Masataka Kosaka. *Soviet Far East Buildup*. Westport, CT: Praeger, 1986.

Soloveitchik, Joseph P. *Visions and Leadership*. New York: Toras Horav Foundation, 2013.

Special to *The New York Times*. "South Africa Seizes Tutu's Passport." https://www.nytimes.com/1981/04/17/world/south-africa-seizes-tutu-s-passport.html.

Spencer, Jonathan, et al. *Checkpoint, Temple, Church and Mosque*. London: Pluto, 2013.

Stack, Peggy Fletcher. "Brigham Young may have started the priesthood ban on blacks, but he was 'no racist,' say his descendants. His 'mission was to save the church.'" https://www.sltrib.com/religion/2018/06/10/brigham-young-may-have-started-the-priesthood-ban-on-blacks-but-he-was-no-racist-say-his-descendants-his-mission-was-to-save-the-church/.

Stampp, Kenneth. *The Peculiar Institution*. New York: Vintage, 1956.

Stearns, Marshall, and Jean Stearns. *Jazz Dance*. New York: Da Capo, 1994.

Taub, Matthew. "'Are We Not American Soldiers?' When the U.S. Military Treated German POWs Better Than Black Troops." https://time.com/5872361/wwii-german-pows-civil-rights/.

Teachingresources.atlas.illinois.edu. "The Chinese Experience in 19th Century America." http://teachingresources.atlas.illinois.edu/chinese_exp/introduction04.html.

Tennent, Timothy C. *Theology in the Context of World Christianity*. Grand Rapids: Zondervan Academic, 2007.

Terry, Walter. *Invitation to Dance*. New York: A. S. Barnes, 1941.

Tharps, Lori L. "The Difference Between Racism and Colorism." https://time.com/4512430/colorism-in-america/.

Thefreedictionary.com. "Truster." https://www.thefreedictionary.com/truster.

Toye, Richard. *Churchill's Empire*. New York: Holt, 2010.

Trewhela, Lee. "Britain's First Black Ballerina." https://www.cornwalllive.com/news/cornwall-news/britains-first-black-ballerina-fought-5162277.

Tuckness, Alex. "Locke's Political Philosophy." https://plato.stanford.edu/entries/locke-political/.

Turner, Edith. *Experiencing Ritual*. Philadelphia: University of Pennsylvania Press, 1992.

Urrrborderland.omeka.net. "White Abolitionists." https://urrrborderland.omeka.net/exhibits/show/ugrr/agents/white-abolitionists.

Uwagba, Otegha. *Whites: On Race and Other Falsehoods*. London: Fourth Estate, 2020.

Vaguelyinteresting.co.uk "The dying nations of the world." https://www.vaguely interesting.co.uk/the-dying-nations-of-the-world/.

Valery, Paul. "Regards sur le monde actuel." https://www.atlasofplaces.com/essays/ regards-sur-le-monde-actuel/.

Van Buren, Paul M. *A Theology of Jewish-Christian Reality Pt. 2*. San Francisco: Harper & Row, 1987.

Volf, Miroslav. *Allah*. New York: HarperOne, 2011.

Vox First Person. "The loneliness of being mixed race in America." https://www.vox. com/first-person/21734156/kamala-harris-mixed-race-biracial-multiracial.

Wade, Peter. *Race*. Cambridge: Cambridge University Press, 2015.

Walker, Adam. "Obedience." https://www.alislam.org/articles/obedience/.

Ward, Graham. *How the Light Gets In*. Oxford: Oxford University Press, 2016.

Waywordradio.org. "Origin of Steppin' and Fetchin'." https://www.waywordradio.org/ origin-of-steppin-and-fetchin/.

Westcott, Ben, and Steven Jiang. "Here's what wolf warrior diplomacy means." https:// www.cnn.com/2020/05/28/asia/china-wolf-warrior-diplomacy-intl-hnk/index. html.

Wikipedia.org. "Bickershaw Festival." https://en.wikipedia.org/wiki/Bickershaw_Festival.

Winton-Henry, Cynthia. *Dance—the Sacred Art*. Nashville: Skylight, 2009.

Wolfe, Patrick. "Race and Citizenship." https://apcentral.collegeboard.org/series/ america-on-the-world-stage/race-and-citizenship.

Worldinprayer.org. "World News This Week in Prayer—Thursday, November 3, 2022." https://worldinprayer.org/2022/world-news-this-week-in-prayer-thursday-nov ember-3-2022/.

Yahya, Samar. "Obedience to Allah." https://saudigazette.com.sa/article/174504.

Printed in Great Britain
by Amazon

36302518R00108